THE
MORNING
JOURNAL

Two Minutes to Start
Your Day with Intention

LEAHANNE THOMAS

STERLING
New York

STERLING ETHOS
New York

STERLING ETHOS and the distinctive Sterling Ethos logo are registered
trademarks of Sterling Publishing Co., Inc.

Text © 2022 Leahanne Thomas

ISBN 978-1-4549-4619-9

Distributed in Canada by Sterling Publishing Co., Inc.
c/o Canadian Manda Group, 664 Annette Street
Toronto, Ontario, Canada M6S 2C8
Distributed in the United Kingdom by GMC Distribution Services
Castle Place, 166 High Street, Lewes, East Sussex, England BN7 1XU
Distributed in Australia by NewSouth Books
University of New South Wales, Sydney, NSW 2052, Australia

For information about custom editions, special sales, and premium
purchases, please contact specialsales@sterlingpublishing.com.

Printed in Malaysia

2 4 6 8 10 9 7 5 3 1

www.sterlingpublishing.com

Design by Jordan Wannemacher

Cover and interior illustrations by Maggie Enterrios
Cover design by Melissa Farris

FOR A GOOD DAY'S WORK

Have you noticed that we just jump into the day, managing all our to dos, and then when we come to the end of the day we wonder, "What just happened? What did I do today?"

The Morning Journal was created to help you set purposeful intentions for your day. No day, no future, is guaranteed to us. We honor the gift of each day by using it well. We use it well by being intentional with our time—using it to learn, to grow, and to become better.

How does this book work? It is a quick way to facilitate an intentional day (get in, get out, and get on with your day), but it also requires some reorienting of how you think and approach your day. You are not making a to-do list. Use this book as a deliberate way to bring happiness, focus, and intention to your life every day.

It's structured to be quick and painless, but at the same time, it's flexible. You have the option to write as much or as little as you need. No one wants to do a lot of work before starting the day, otherwise you'd never get out the door. You can also put this journal right next to your desk or workstation to quickly ground and frame your day before you begin.

Each day has four boxes that are "quick hits." First, you tackle anything that may be plaguing your mind—maybe a worry or an unsettled relationship. Negative thoughts or worries can dramatically affect your day without you realizing it.

Then there is a place for an action step to do something to address the worry. Anxiety comes from lack of control, and creating an action step, however small, gives you some control back.

Then move on to happiness and gratitude and service. This helps ground you in positive thinking and action, which is the most important tool for success and happiness each and every day. Did you notice the sunshine on your walk outside? Did someone share a kind word?

The weekend is an opportunity to reflect on the past week and to rejuvenate and prepare for the week ahead. You have a quick way to capture your most positive experience during the week and then set some intentions for fun and relaxation but also intentional connections with others.

Quarterly, instead of a weekend page, there is a reflection page to look back on the last few months. What, if anything, has changed for you since you have been more intentional in your life? Maybe you see things differently or you have a new focus. It's also a time for acknowledging progress, through accomplishments, skills you have developed through practice and relationships that have gotten stronger because of focus.

And that's it. If you commit to five minutes every morning before you turn on your computer or scroll through your phone, you will be stronger, more in control, happier, and feel like you're making more deliberate progress in your life.

I hope you like this journal; I made it for you.

—LEAHANNE

DATE: __/__/__

"There are two ways of spreading light: to be the candle or the mirror that reflects it."
—EDITH WHARTON

One hope I have for the future:

One step I can take toward that goal:

One act of service I can provide today:

One aspiration I have today:

☐ Being slow & deliberate
☐ Being quick & decisive
☐ Listening without judging
☐ Taking action on ideas
☐ Being responsive
☐ Being forgiving
☐ Other:

DATE: __/__/__

"A strong, positive self-image is the best possible preparation for success."
—JOYCE BROTHERS

Best encounter of the week:

One fun thing I want to do this weekend:

One to-do item I want to accomplish:

One person I want to engage with:

DATE: __/__/__

"Clouds come floating into my life, no longer to carry rain or usher storm, but to add color to my sunset sky." —**RABINDRANATH TAGORE**

One thing that is worrying me today:

One step I can take to address my worry:

One thing I am grateful for today:

One aspiration I have today:

- ☐ Patience & understanding
- ☐ Follow-through & accountability
- ☐ Communicating my feelings
- ☐ Allowing discomfort
- ☐ Being vulnerable
- ☐ Baking a risk
- ☐ Other:

"No matter what you're going through, there's a light at the end of the tunnel . . . just keep working toward it and you'll find the positive side of things."
—DEMI LOVATO

DATE: ___/___/___

One relationship that is unsettled:

One change I can make to improve it:

One beautiful thing I notice:

One happiness I can claim today:

- ☐ Meditation or prayer
- ☐ Exercise
- ☐ Hobby
- ☐ Act of service
- ☐ Act of kindness
- ☐ Being in nature
- ☐ Other:

DATE: ___/___/___

"Perfection is not attainable, but if we chase perfection, we can catch excellence."
—VINCE LOMBARDI

One thing I want to get better at:

One step I can take to do that:

One act of kindness I can do today:

One aspiration I have today:

☐ Being healthy & active
☐ Being caring & considerate
☐ Actively engaging with others
☐ Being reflective
☐ Being quiet
☐ Asking for what I need

"I think anything is possible if you have the mindset and the will and desire to do it and put the time in." —**ROGER CLEMENS**

DATE: ___/___/___

One relationship I am neglecting:

One change I can make to improve it:

One beautiful thing I notice:

One happiness I can claim today:

☐ Meditation or prayer
☐ Exercise
☐ Hobby
☐ Act of service
☐ Act of kindness
☐ Being in nature
☐ Other:

"Not on one strand are all life's jewels strung." —**WILLIAM MORRIS**

DATE: ___/___/___

One hope I have for the future:

One step I can take toward that goal:

One act of service I can provide today:

One aspiration I have today:

☐ Being slow & deliberate
☐ Being quick & decisive
☐ Listening without judging
☐ Taking action on ideas
☐ Being responsive
☐ Being forgiving

"If you believe in yourself and have dedication and pride—and never quit, you'll be a winner. The price of victory is high but so are the rewards."
—PAUL "BEAR" BRYANT

Best encounter of the week:

One fun thing I want to do this weekend:

One to-do item I want to accomplish:

One person I want to engage with:

DATE: ___/___/___

"Every day brings new choices." —**MARTHA BECK**

One thing that is worrying
me today:

One step I can take to address
my worry:

One thing I am grateful for today:

One aspiration I have today:

☐ Patience & understanding
☐ Follow-through &
   accountability
☐ Communicating my feelings
☐ Allowing discomfort
☐ Being vulnerable
☐ Taking a risk

DATE: __/__/__

"We know what we are, but know not what we may be." **—WILLIAM SHAKESPEARE**

One relationship that is unsettled:

One change I can make to improve it:

One beautiful thing I notice:

One happiness I can claim today:

☐ Meditation or prayer
☐ Exercise
☐ Hobby
☐ Act of service
☐ Act of kindness
☐ Being in nature
☐ Other:

DATE: __/__/__

"It's a wonderful thing to be optimistic. It keeps you healthy and it keeps you resilient."
—DANIEL KAHNERMAN

One thing I want to get better at:

One step I can take to do that:

One act of kindness I can do today:

One aspiration I have today:

- ☐ Being healthy & active
- ☐ Being caring & considerate
- ☐ Actively engaging with others
- ☐ Being reflective
- ☐ Being quiet
- ☐ Asking for what I need
- ☐ Other

DATE: ___/___/___

"It is during our darkest moments that we must focus to see the light." —**ARISTOTLE ONASSIS**

One relationship I am neglecting:

One change I can make to improve it:

One beautiful thing I notice:

One happiness I can claim today:

- ☐ Meditation or prayer
- ☐ Exercise
- ☐ Hobby
- ☐ Act of service
- ☐ Act of kindness
- ☐ Being in nature
- ☐ Other:

DATE: __/__/__

"Always turn a negative situation into a positive situation." —**MICHAEL JORDAN**

One hope I have for the future:

One step I can take toward that goal:

One act of service I can provide today:

One aspiration I have today:

☐ Being slow & deliberate
☐ Being quick & decisive
☐ Listening without judging
☐ Taking action on ideas
☐ Being responsive
☐ Being forgiving

DATE: __/__/__

"Don't judge each day by the harvest you reap but by the seeds that you plant."
—ROBERT LOUIS STEVENSON

Best encounter of the week:

One fun thing I want to do this weekend:

One to-do item I want to accomplish:

One person I want to engage with:

"If I do nothing, if I study nothing, if I cease searching, then, woe is me, I am lost. That is how I look at it—keep going . . . come what may."
—VINCENT VAN GOGH

One thing that is worrying me today:

One step I can take to address my worry:

One thing I am grateful for today:

One aspiration I have today:

☐ Patience & understanding
☐ Follow-through & accountability
☐ Communicating my feelings
☐ Allowing discomfort
☐ Being vulnerable
☐ Taking a risk
☐ Other:

"I hated every minute of training, but I said, 'Don't quit. Suffer now and live the rest of your life as a champion.'" **—MUHAMMAD ALI**

TUESDAY

DATE: ___/___/___

One relationship that is unsettled:

One change I can make to improve it:

One beautiful thing I notice:

One happiness I can claim today:

☐ Meditation or prayer
☐ Exercise
☐ Hobby
☐ Act of service
☐ Act of kindness
☐ Being in nature
☐ Other:

DATE: __/__/__

"If you're not making mistakes, then you're not doing anything. I'm positive that a doer makes mistakes." —**JOHN WOODEN**

One thing I want to get better at:

One step I can take to do that:

One act of kindness I can do today:

One aspiration I have today:

- ☐ Being healthy & active
- ☐ Being caring & considerate
- ☐ Actively engaging with others
- ☐ Being reflective
- ☐ Being quiet
- ☐ Asking for what I need
- ☐ Other

DATE: __/__/__

"What lies behind you and what lies in front of you, pales in comparison to what lies inside of you." —**RALPH WALDO EMERSON**

One relationship I am neglecting:

One change I can make to improve it:

One beautiful thing I notice:

One happiness I can claim today:

- ☐ Meditation or prayer
- ☐ Exercise
- ☐ Hobby
- ☐ Act of service
- ☐ Act of kindness
- ☐ Being in nature
- ☐ Other:

"Always do your best. Your best is going to change from moment to moment. . . . Under any circumstance, simply do your best."
—DON MIGUEL RUIZ

One hope I have for the future:

One step I can take toward that goal:

One act of service I can provide today:

One aspiration I have today:

- ☐ Being slow & deliberate
- ☐ Being quick & decisive
- ☐ Listening without judging
- ☐ Taking action on ideas
- ☐ Being responsive
- ☐ Being forgiving
- ☐ Other:

DATE: __/__/__

"No act of kindness, no matter how small, is ever wasted." —**AESOP**

Best encounter of the week:

One fun thing I want to do this weekend:

One to-do item I want to accomplish:

One person I want to engage with:

DATE: __/__/__

"A good laugh is sunshine in the house."
—WILLIAM MAKEPEACE THACKERAY

One thing that is worrying
me today:

One step I can take to address
my worry:

One thing I am grateful for today:

One aspiration I have today:

☐ Patience & understanding
☐ Follow-through &
   accountability
☐ Communicating my feelings
☐ Allowing discomfort
☐ Being vulnerable
☐ Taking a risk
☐ Other:

"We must get rid of the life we have planned, so as to have the life that is waiting for us."
—**JOSEPH CAMPBELL**

One relationship that is unsettled:

One change I can make to improve it:

One beautiful thing I notice:

One happiness I can claim today:

☐ Meditation or prayer
☐ Exercise
☐ Hobby
☐ Act of service
☐ Act of kindness
☐ Being in nature
☐ Other:

DATE: __/__/__

"I must trust that the little bit of love that I sow now will bear many fruits, here in this world and the life to come." —**HENRI NOUWEN**

One thing I want to get better at:

One step I can take to do that:

One act of kindness I can do today:

One aspiration I have today:

- ☐ Being healthy & active
- ☐ Being caring & considerate
- ☐ Actively engaging with others
- ☐ Being reflective
- ☐ Being quiet
- ☐ Asking for what I need
- ☐ Other:

DATE: __/__/__

"Every morning when I wake up I can choose joy, happiness, negativity, pain." —**KEVYN AUCOIN**

One relationship I am neglecting:

One change I can make to improve it:

One beautiful thing I notice:

One happiness I can claim today:

☐ Meditation or prayer
☐ Exercise
☐ Hobby
☐ Act of service
☐ Act of kindness
☐ Being in nature
☐ Other:

DATE: __/__/__

"Work hard, stay positive, and get up early. It's the best part of the day."
—GEORGE ALLEN SR.

One hope I have for the future:

One step I can take toward that goal:

One act of service I can provide today:

One aspiration I have today:
- ☐ Being slow & deliberate
- ☐ Being quick & decisive
- ☐ Listening without judging
- ☐ Taking action on ideas
- ☐ Being responsive
- ☐ Being forgiving
- ☐ Other:

DATE: __/__/__

"The part of being happy lies in the power of extracting happiness from common things."
—HENRY WARD BEECHER

Best encounter of the week:

One fun thing I want to do this weekend:

One to-do item I want to accomplish:

One person I want to engage with:

"Your smile will give you a positive countenance that will make people feel comfortable around you."
—LES BROWN

DATE: __/__/__

One thing that is worrying me today:

One step I can take to address my worry:

One thing I am grateful for today:

One aspiration I have today:

☐ Patience & understanding
☐ Follow-through & accountability
☐ Communicating my feelings
☐ Allowing discomfort
☐ Being vulnerable
☐ Taking a risk
☐ Other:

"Ah, but a man's reach should exceed his grasp, or what's a heaven for?" —**ROBERT BROWNING**

DATE: ___/___/___

One relationship that is unsettled:

One change I can make to improve it:

One beautiful thing I notice:

One happiness I can claim today:

☐ Meditation or prayer
☐ Exercise
☐ Hobby
☐ Act of service
☐ Act of kindness
☐ Being in nature
☐ Other:

DATE: __/__/__

"To succeed, you need to find something to hold on to, something to motivate you, something to inspire you." **—TONY DORSETT**

One thing I want to get better at:

One step I can take to do that:

One act of kindness I can do today:

One aspiration I have today:

☐ Being healthy & active
☐ Being caring & considerate
☐ Actively engaging with others
☐ Being reflective
☐ Being quiet
☐ Asking for what I need
☐ Other:

DATE: __/__/__

"If I have seen further than others, it is by standing upon the shoulders of giants."
—ISAAC NEWTON

One relationship I am neglecting:

One change I can make to improve it:

One beautiful thing I notice:

One happiness I can claim today:

☐ Meditation or prayer
☐ Exercise
☐ Hobby
☐ Act of service
☐ Act of kindness
☐ Being in nature
☐ Other:

DATE: ___/___/___

"*There is no greater joy than to have an endlessly changing horizon, for each day to have a new and different sun.*" —**CHRISTOPHER MCCANDLESS**

One hope I have for the future:

One step I can take toward that goal:

One act of service I can provide today:

One aspiration I have today:

- ☐ Being slow & deliberate
- ☐ Being quick & decisive
- ☐ Listening without judging
- ☐ Taking action on ideas
- ☐ Being responsive
- ☐ Being forgiving
- ☐ Other:

"If opportunity doesn't knock, build a door."
—MILTON BERLE

Best encounter of the week:

One fun thing I want to do this weekend:

One to-do item I want to accomplish:

One person I want to engage with:

"If you have a positive attitude and constantly strive to give your best effort, eventually you will overcome your immediate problems and find you are ready for greater challenges." —**PAT RILEY**

One thing that is worrying me today:

One step I can take to address my worry:

One thing I am grateful for today:

One aspiration I have today:

☐ Patience & understanding
☐ Follow-through & accountability
☐ Communicating my feelings
☐ Allowing discomfort
☐ Being vulnerable
☐ Taking a risk

*"Let us remember; One book, one pen, one child,
and one teacher can change the world."*
—MALALA YOUSAFZAI

DATE: ___/___/___

One relationship that is unsettled:

One change I can make to improve it:

One beautiful thing I notice:

One happiness I can claim today:

☐ Meditation or prayer
☐ Exercise
☐ Hobby
☐ Act of service
☐ Act of kindness
☐ Being in nature
☐ Other:

"Positive thinking will let you do everything better than negative thinking will." —**ZIG ZIGLAR**

DATE: ___/___/___

One thing I want to get better at:

One step I can take to do that:

One act of kindness I can do today:

One aspiration I have today:

☐ Being healthy & active
☐ Being caring & considerate
☐ Actively engaging with others
☐ Being reflective
☐ Being quiet
☐ Asking for what I need
☐ Other:

"It's never too late to be what you might have been." **—GEORGE ELIOT**

DATE: __/__/__

One relationship I am neglecting:

One change I can make to improve it:

One beautiful thing I notice:

One happiness I can claim today:

- ☐ Meditation or prayer
- ☐ Exercise
- ☐ Hobby
- ☐ Act of service
- ☐ Act of kindness
- ☐ Being in nature
- ☐ Other:

DATE: ___/___/___

"A world full of happiness is not beyond human power to create." —**BERTRAND RUSSELL**

One hope I have for the future:

One step I can take toward that goal:

One act of service I can provide today:

One aspiration I have today:

- ☐ Being slow & deliberate
- ☐ Being quick & decisive
- ☐ Listening without judging
- ☐ Taking action on ideas
- ☐ Being responsive
- ☐ Being forgiving
- ☐ Other:

"Happiness is a butterfly which, when pursued, is always beyond your grasp, but which, if you will sit down quietly, may alight upon you."
—ANONYMOUS

Best encounter of the week:

One fun thing I want to do this weekend:

One to-do item I want to accomplish:

One person I want to engage with:

DATE: ___/___/___

"The person who can bring the spirit of laughter into a room is indeed blessed."
—BENNETT CERF

One thing that is worrying me today:

One step I can take to address my worry:

One thing I am grateful for today:

One aspiration I have today:

- ☐ Patience & understanding
- ☐ Follow-through & accountability
- ☐ Communicating my feelings
- ☐ Allowing discomfort
- ☐ Being vulnerable
- ☐ Taking a risk
- ☐ Other:

DATE: __/__/__

"Put your heart, mind, and soul into even your smallest acts. This is the secret of success."
—SIVANANDA SARASWATI

One relationship that is unsettled:

One change I can make to improve it:

One beautiful thing I notice:

One happiness I can claim today:

☐ Meditation or prayer
☐ Exercise
☐ Hobby
☐ Act of service
☐ Act of kindness
☐ Being in nature
☐ Other:

DATE: ___/___/___

"Our happiness depends on the mind which is within us, and not on the circumstances which are without us." **—THOMAS CARLYLE**

One thing I want to get better at:

One step I can take to do that:

One act of kindness I can do today:

One aspiration I have today:

- ☐ Being healthy & active
- ☐ Being caring & considerate
- ☐ Actively engaging with others
- ☐ Being reflective
- ☐ Being quiet
- ☐ Asking for what I need
- ☐ Other:

DATE: ___/___/___

"Change your thoughts and you change your world." —**NORMAN VINCENT PEALE**

One relationship I am neglecting:

One change I can make to improve it:

One beautiful thing I notice:

One happiness I can claim today:

☐ Meditation or prayer
☐ Exercise
☐ Hobby
☐ Act of service
☐ Act of kindness
☐ Being in nature
☐ Other:

DATE: ___/___/___

"Your present circumstances don't determine where you can go; they merely determine where you start." **—NIDO QUBEIN**

One hope I have for the future:

One step I can take toward that goal:

One act of service I can provide today:

One aspiration I have today:

☐ Being slow & deliberate
☐ Being quick & decisive
☐ Listening without judging
☐ Taking action on ideas
☐ Being responsive
☐ Being forgiving
☐ Other:

"Correction does much, but encouragement does more."

—JOHANN WOLFGANG VON GOETHE

Best encounter of the week:

One fun thing I want to do this weekend:

One to-do item I want to accomplish:

One person I want to engage with:

> *"When you get into a tight place [and] it seems as though you could not hang on a minute longer, never give up then, for that is just the place and time that the tide'll turn."*
> **—HARRIET BEECHER STOWE**

One thing that is worrying me today:

One step I can take to address my worry:

One thing I am grateful for today:

One aspiration I have today:

☐ Patience & understanding
☐ Follow-through & accountability
☐ Communicating my feelings
☐ Allowing discomfort
☐ Being vulnerable
☐ Taking a risk
☐ Other:

"Happiness is a direction, not a place."
—SYDNEY J. HARRIS

One relationship that is unsettled:

One change I can make to improve it:

One beautiful thing I notice:

One happiness I can claim today:

- ☐ Meditation or prayer
- ☐ Exercise
- ☐ Hobby
- ☐ Act of service
- ☐ Act of kindness
- ☐ Being in nature
- ☐ Other:

"No matter what people tell you, words and ideas can change the world." —**ROBIN WILLIAMS**

DATE: ___/___/___

One thing I want to get better at:

One step I can take to do that:

One act of kindness I can do today:

One aspiration I have today:
☐ Being healthy & active
☐ Being caring & considerate
☐ Actively engaging with others
☐ Being reflective
☐ Being quiet
☐ Asking for what I need
☐ Other:

DATE: ___/___/___

"I believe if you keep your faith, you keep your trust, you keep the right attitude, if you're grateful, you'll see God open new doors." **—JOEL OSTEEN**

One relationship I am neglecting:

One change I can make to improve it:

One beautiful thing I notice:

One happiness I can claim today:

- ☐ Meditation or prayer
- ☐ Exercise
- ☐ Hobby
- ☐ Act of service
- ☐ Act of kindness
- ☐ Being in nature
- ☐ Other:

One hope I have for the future:

One step I can take toward that goal:

One act of service I can provide today:

One aspiration I have today:

☐ Being slow & deliberate
☐ Being quick & decisive
☐ Listening without judging
☐ Taking action on ideas
☐ Being responsive
☐ Being forgiving
☐ Other:

*"Action may not always bring happiness;
but there is no happiness without action."*
—BENJAMIN DISRAELI

DATE: __/__/__

Best encounter of the week:

One fun thing I want to do this weekend:

One to-do item I want to accomplish:

One person I want to engage with:

DATE: __/__/__

"You don't look out here for God, something in the sky, you look in you." —**ALAN WATTS**

One thing that is worrying me today:

One step I can take to address my worry:

One thing I am grateful for today:

One aspiration I have today:

- ☐ Patience & understanding
- ☐ Follow-through & accountability
- ☐ Communicating my feelings
- ☐ Allowing discomfort
- ☐ Being vulnerable
- ☐ Taking a risk
- ☐ Other:

"If a man does not keep pace with his companions, perhaps it is because he hears a different drummer. Let him step to the music which he hears, however measured or far away."
—HENRY DAVID THOREAU

One relationship that is unsettled:

One change I can make to improve it:

One beautiful thing I notice:

One happiness I can claim today:

☐ Meditation or prayer
☐ Exercise
☐ Hobby
☐ Act of service
☐ Act of kindness
☐ Being in nature
☐ Other:

DATE: __/__/__

*"You cannot have a positive life and a
negative mind."* —**JOYCE MEYER**

One thing I want to get better at:

One step I can take to do that:

One act of kindness I can
do today:

One aspiration I have today:

☐ Being healthy & active
☐ Being caring & considerate
☐ Actively engaging with
   others
☐ Being reflective
☐ Being quiet
☐ Asking for what I need
☐ Other:

DATE: __/__/__

"The most authentic thing about us is our capacity to create, to overcome, to endure, toto transform, to love, and to be greater than our suffering." **—BEN OKRI**

One relationship I am neglecting:

One change I can make to improve it:

One beautiful thing I notice:

One happiness I can claim today:

☐ Meditation or prayer
☐ Exercise
☐ Hobby
☐ Act of service
☐ Act of kindness
☐ Being in nature
☐ Other:

DATE: ___/___/___

"Happiness is not a matter of intensity but of balance, order, rhythm and harmony."
—THOMAS MERTON

One hope I have for the future:

One step I can take toward that goal:

One act of service I can provide today:

One aspiration I have today:

☐ Being slow & deliberate
☐ Being quick & decisive
☐ Listening without judging
☐ Taking action on ideas
☐ Being responsive
☐ Being forgiving
☐ Other:

"The only journey is the one within."
—RAINER MARIA RILKE

Best encounter of the week:

One fun thing I want to do this weekend:

One to-do item I want to accomplish:

One person I want to engage with:

"I believe in karma, and I believe if you put out positive vibes to everybody, that's all you're going to get back." —**KESHA**

One thing that is worrying me today:

One step I can take to address my worry:

One thing I am grateful for today:

One aspiration I have today:

- ☐ Patience & understanding
- ☐ Follow-through & accountability
- ☐ Communicating my feelings
- ☐ Allowing discomfort
- ☐ Being vulnerable
- ☐ Taking a risk
- ☐ Other:

DATE: __/__/__

"Tears of joy are like the summer raindrops pierced by sunbeams." **—HOSEA BALLOU**

One relationship that is unsettled:

One change I can make to improve it:

One beautiful thing I notice:

One happiness I can claim today:

☐ Meditation or prayer
☐ Exercise
☐ Hobby
☐ Act of service
☐ Act of kindness
☐ Being in nature
☐ Other:

DATE: ___/___/___

"In order to carry a positive action we must develop here a positive vision."
—TENZIN GYATSO, THE 14TH DALAI LAMA

One thing I want to get better at:

One step I can take to do that:

One act of kindness I can do today:

One aspiration I have today:

- ☐ Being healthy & active
- ☐ Being caring & considerate
- ☐ Actively engaging with others
- ☐ Being reflective
- ☐ Being quiet
- ☐ Asking for what I need
- ☐ Other:

"My mission in life is not merely to survive, but to thrive; and to do so with some passion, some compassion, some humor, and some style."
—**MAYA ANGELOU**

One relationship I am neglecting:

One change I can make to improve it:

One beautiful thing I notice:

One happiness I can claim today:

☐ Meditation or prayer
☐ Exercise
☐ Hobby
☐ Act of service
☐ Act of kindness
☐ Being in nature
☐ Other:

*"Always go into meetings or negotiations with
a positive attitude. Tell yourself you're going to
make this the best deal for all parties."*
—NATALIE MASSENET

One hope I have for the future:

One step I can take toward
that goal:

One act of service I can
provide today:

One aspiration I have today:

☐ Being slow & deliberate
☐ Being quick & decisive
☐ Listening without judging
☐ Taking action on ideas
☐ Being responsive
☐ Being forgiving
☐ Other:

"*Keep your feet on the ground, but let your heart soar as high as it will. Refuse to be average or to surrender to the chill of your spiritual environment.*" —**ARTHUR HELPS**

Best encounter of the week

One fun thing I want to do this weekend:

One to-do item I want to accomplish:

One person I want to engage with:

DATE: ___/___/___

"*There is a divine purpose in the adversities we encounter every day. They prepare, they purge, they purify, and thus they bless.*" —**JAMES E. FAUST**

One thing that is worrying me today:

One step I can take to address my worry:

One thing I am grateful for today:

One aspiration I have today:

☐ Patience & understanding
☐ Follow-through & accountability
☐ Communicating my feelings
☐ Allowing discomfort
☐ Being vulnerable
☐ Taking a risk
☐ Other:

DATE: ___/___/___

"Positive anything is better than negative nothing."
—ELBERT HUBBARD

One relationship that is unsettled:

One change I can make to improve it:

One beautiful thing I notice:

One happiness I can claim today:

☐ Meditation or prayer
☐ Exercise
☐ Hobby
☐ Act of service
☐ Act of kindness
☐ Being in nature
☐ Other:

"Somewhere, something incredible is waiting to be known." **—SHARON BEGLEY**

One thing I want to get better at:

One step I can take to do that:

One act of kindness I can do today:

One aspiration I have today:

- ☐ Being healthy & active
- ☐ Being caring & considerate
- ☐ Actively engaging with others
- ☐ Being reflective
- ☐ Being quiet
- ☐ Asking for what I need
- ☐ Other:

"*Trust in dreams, for in them is hidden the gate to eternity.*" —**KHALIL GIBRAN**

One relationship I am neglecting:

One change I can make to improve it:

One beautiful thing I notice:

One happiness I can claim today:

☐ Meditation or prayer
☐ Exercise
☐ Hobby
☐ Act of service
☐ Act of kindness
☐ Being in nature
☐ Other:

"Just don't give up trying to do what you really want to do. Where there is love and inspiration, I don't think you can go wrong."
—ELLA FITZGERALD

DATE: __/__/__

One hope I have for the future:

One step I can take toward that goal:

One act of service I can provide today:

One aspiration I have today:

- ☐ Being slow & deliberate
- ☐ Being quick & decisive
- ☐ Listening without judging
- ☐ Taking action on ideas
- ☐ Being responsive
- ☐ Being forgiving

A TIME TO REVIEW

DATE: __/__/__

What have I accomplished?

What has changed about me?

What have I gotten better at?

What person have I gotten closer to?

"Happiness resides not in possession and not in gold; happiness dwells in the soul."
—DEMOCRITUS

One thing that is worrying me today:

One step I can take to address my worry:

One thing I am grateful for today:

One aspiration I have today:

☐ Patience & understanding
☐ Follow-through & accountability
☐ Communicating my feelings
☐ Allowing discomfort
☐ Being vulnerable
☐ Taking a risk
☐ Other:

DATE: __/__/__

"Today or any day that phone may ring and bring good news." —**ETHEL WATERS**

One relationship that is unsettled:

One change I can make to improve it:

One beautiful thing I notice:

One happiness I can claim today:

- ☐ Meditation or prayer
- ☐ Exercise
- ☐ Hobby
- ☐ Act of service
- ☐ Act of kindness
- ☐ Being in nature
- ☐ Other:

DATE: __/__/__

"Try to be a rainbow in someone's cloud."
—MAYA ANGELOU

One thing I want to get better at:

One step I can take to do that:

One act of kindness I can
do today:

One aspiration I have today:

☐ Being healthy & active
☐ Being caring & considerate
☐ Actively engaging with
   others
☐ Being reflective
☐ Being quiet
☐ Asking for what I need
☐ Other:

"When you show deep empathy toward others, their defensive energy goes down, and positive energy replaces it." **—STEPHEN COVEY**

DATE: __/__/__

One relationship I am neglecting:

One change I can make to improve it:

One beautiful thing I notice:

One happiness I can claim today:

☐ Meditation or prayer
☐ Exercise
☐ Hobby
☐ Act of service
☐ Act of kindness
☐ Being in nature
☐ Other:

DATE: __/__/__

"If there were no night, we would not appreciate the day, nor could we see the stars and the vastness of the heavens. We must partake the bitter with the sweet." —**JAMES E. FAUST**

One hope I have for the future:

One step I can take toward that goal:

One act of service I can provide today:

One aspiration I have today:

☐ Being slow & deliberate
☐ Being quick & decisive
☐ Listening without judging
☐ Taking action on ideas
☐ Being responsive
☐ Being forgiving
☐ Other:

"I do believe we are all connected. I do believe in positive energy. I do believe in putting good out into the world. And I believe in taking care of each other." **—HARVEY FIERSTEIN**

DATE: __/__/__

Best encounter of the week:

One fun thing I want to do this weekend:

One to-do item I want to accomplish:

One person I want to engage with:

"Give light and people will find the way."
—ELLA BAKER

DATE: ___/___/___

One thing that is worrying
me today:

One step I can take to address
my worry:

One thing I am grateful for today:

One aspiration I have today:

- ☐ Patience & understanding
- ☐ Follow-through &
  accountability
- ☐ Communicating my feelings
- ☐ Allowing discomfort
- ☐ Being vulnerable
- ☐ Taking a risk
- ☐ Other:

"My purpose: to lift your spirit and to motivate you." —**MAVIS STAPLES**

DATE: __/__/__

One relationship that is unsettled:

One change I can make to improve it:

One beautiful thing I notice:

One happiness I can claim today:

- ☐ Meditation or prayer
- ☐ Exercise
- ☐ Hobby
- ☐ Act of service
- ☐ Act of kindness
- ☐ Being in nature
- ☐ Other:

DATE: ___/___/___

"Light tomorrow with today!"
—ELIZABETH BARRETT BROWNING

One thing I want to get better at:

One step I can take to do that:

One act of kindness I can do today:

One aspiration I have today:

☐ Being healthy & active
☐ Being caring & considerate
☐ Actively engaging with others
☐ Being reflective
☐ Being quiet
☐ Asking for what I need
☐ Other:

DATE: __/__/__

"When you are enthusiastic about what you do, you feel this positive energy. It's very simple."
—PAULO COELHO

One relationship I am neglecting:

One change I can make to improve it:

One beautiful thing I notice:

One happiness I can claim today:

- ☐ Meditation or prayer
- ☐ Exercise
- ☐ Hobby
- ☐ Act of service
- ☐ Act of kindness
- ☐ Being in nature
- ☐ Other:

"Every story I create, creates me. I write to create myself." **—OCTAVIA E. BUTLER**

DATE: __/__/__

One hope I have for the future:

One step I can take toward that goal:

One act of service I can provide today:

One aspiration I have today:

- ☐ Being slow & deliberate
- ☐ Being quick & decisive
- ☐ Listening without judging
- ☐ Taking action on ideas
- ☐ Being responsive
- ☐ Being forgiving
- ☐ Other:

*"True happiness is . . . to enjoy the present,
without anxious dependence upon the future."*
—SENECA

Best encounter of the week:

One fun thing I want to do this
weekend:

One to-do item I want to
accomplish:

One person I want to engage with:

DATE: __/__/__

"A champion is someone who gets up when he can't." —**JACK DEMPSEY**

One thing that is worrying me today:

One step I can take to address my worry:

One thing I am grateful for today:

One aspiration I have today:

- ☐ Patience & understanding
- ☐ Follow-through & accountability
- ☐ Communicating my feelings
- ☐ Allowing discomfort
- ☐ Being vulnerable
- ☐ Taking a risk
- ☐ Other:

DATE: ___/___/___

"Say and do something positive that will help the situation; it doesn't take any brains to complain." —**ROBERT A. COOK**

One relationship that is unsettled:

One change I can make to improve it:

One beautiful thing I notice:

One happiness I can claim today:

☐ Meditation or prayer
☐ Exercise
☐ Hobby
☐ Act of service
☐ Act of kindness
☐ Being in nature
☐ Other:

DATE: ___/___/___

"Out of difficulties grow miracles."
—JEAN DE LA BRUYÈRE

One thing I want to get better at:

One step I can take to do that:

One act of kindness I can
do today:

One aspiration I have today:

☐ Being healthy & active
☐ Being caring & considerate
☐ Actively engaging with
   others
☐ Being reflective
☐ Being quiet
☐ Asking for what I need
☐ Other:

"The best thing to do when you find yourself in a hurting or vulnerable place is to surround yourself with the strongest, finest, most positive people you know." **—KRISTIN ARMSTRONG**

One relationship I am neglecting:

One change I can make to improve it:

One beautiful thing I notice:

One happiness I can claim today:

☐ Meditation or prayer
☐ Exercise
☐ Hobby
☐ Act of service
☐ Act of kindness
☐ Being in nature
☐ Other:

DATE: __/__/__

"I believe every human being has a finite number of heartbeats. I don't intend to waste any of mine."
—NEIL ARMSTRONG

One hope I have for the future:

One step I can take toward that goal:

One act of service I can provide today:

One aspiration I have today:

☐ Being slow & deliberate
☐ Being quick & decisive
☐ Listening without judging
☐ Taking action on ideas
☐ Being responsive
☐ Being forgiving
☐ Other:

"You're going to go through tough times—that's life. But I say, 'nothing happens to you, it happens for you.' See the positive in negative events."
–JOEL OSTEEN

DATE: __/__/__

Best encounter of the week:

One fun thing I want to do this weekend:

One to-do item I want to accomplish:

One person I want to engage with:

"Someone is sitting in the shade today because someone planted a tree a long time ago."
—**WARREN BUFFETT**

DATE: ___/___/___

One thing that is worrying
me today:

One step I can take to address
my worry:

One thing I am grateful for today:

One aspiration I have today:

- ☐ Patience & understanding
- ☐ Follow-through &
  accountability
- ☐ Communicating my feelings
- ☐ Allowing discomfort
- ☐ Being vulnerable
- ☐ Taking a risk
- ☐ Other:

DATE: ___/___/___

"*I think a lot of times we don't pay enough
attention to people with a positive attitude because
we assume they are naive or stupid or unschooled.*"
—AMY ADAMS

One relationship that is unsettled:

One change I can make to improve it:

One beautiful thing I notice:

One happiness I can claim today:

- ☐ Meditation or prayer
- ☐ Exercise
- ☐ Hobby
- ☐ Act of service
- ☐ Act of kindness
- ☐ Being in nature
- ☐ Other:

DATE: __/__/__

"Do your little bit of good where you are; it's those little bits of good put together that overwhelm the world." —**DESMOND TUTU**

One thing I want to get better at:

One step I can take to do that:

One act of kindness I can do today:

One aspiration I have today:

☐ Being healthy & active
☐ Being caring & considerate
☐ Actively engaging with others
☐ Being reflective
☐ Being quiet
☐ Asking for what I need
☐ Other:

DATE: __/__/__

"Keep your face to the sunshine and you cannot see a shadow." —**HELEN KELLER**

One relationship I am neglecting:

One change I can make to improve it:

One beautiful thing I notice:

One happiness I can claim today:

- ☐ Meditation or prayer
- ☐ Exercise
- ☐ Hobby
- ☐ Act of service
- ☐ Act of kindness
- ☐ Being in nature
- ☐ Other:

DATE: __/__/__

"Nothing is impossible, the word itself says 'I'm possible'!" —**AUDREY HEPBURN**

One hope I have for the future:

One step I can take toward that goal:

One act of service I can provide today:

One aspiration I have today:

- ☐ Being slow & deliberate
- ☐ Being quick & decisive
- ☐ Listening without judging
- ☐ Taking action on ideas
- ☐ Being responsive
- ☐ Being forgiving
- ☐ Other:

DATE: __/__/__

"*A positive attitude is something everyone can work on, and everyone can learn how to employ it.*" –**JOAN LUNDEN**

Best encounter of the week:

One fun thing I want to do this weekend:

One to-do item I want to accomplish:

One person I want to engage with:

DATE: __/__/__

"Learning how to be still, to really be still and let life happen—that stillness becomes a radiance."
—MORGAN FREEMAN

One thing that is worrying me today:

One step I can take to address my worry:

One thing I am grateful for today:

One aspiration I have today:

☐ Patience & understanding
☐ Follow-through & accountability
☐ Communicating my feelings
☐ Allowing discomfort
☐ Being vulnerable
☐ Taking a risk

DATE: ___/___/___

"*I like to encourage people to realize that any action is a good action if it's proactive and there's positive intent behind it.*" —**MICHAEL J. FOX**

One relationship that is unsettled:

One change I can make to improve it:

One beautiful thing I notice:

One happiness I can claim today:

☐ Meditation or prayer
☐ Exercise
☐ Hobby
☐ Act of service
☐ Act of kindness
☐ Being in nature
☐ Other:

"The measure of who we are is what we do with what we have." **—VINCE LOMBARDI**

DATE: __/__/__

One thing I want to get better at:

One step I can take to do that:

One act of kindness I can do today:

One aspiration I have today:

☐ Being healthy & active
☐ Being caring & considerate
☐ Actively engaging with others
☐ Being reflective
☐ Being quiet
☐ Asking for what I need

"Curiosity is one of the permanent and certain characteristics of a vigorous intellect."
—SAMUEL JOHNSON

DATE: __/__/__

One relationship I am neglecting:

One change I can make to improve it:

One beautiful thing I notice:

One happiness I can claim today:

☐ Meditation or prayer
☐ Exercise
☐ Hobby
☐ Act of service
☐ Act of kindness
☐ Being in nature
☐ Other:

"Two roads diverged in a wood, and I—
I took the one less traveled by,
And that has made all the difference."
—ROBERT FROST

One hope I have for the future:

One step I can take toward
that goal:

One act of service I can
provide today:

One aspiration I have today:

☐ Being slow & deliberate
☐ Being quick & decisive
☐ Listening without judging
☐ Taking action on ideas
☐ Being responsive
☐ Being forgiving

DATE: __/__/__

"People deal too much with the negative, with what is wrong. Why not try and see positive things, to just touch those things and make them bloom?"
—THICH NHAT HANH

Best encounter of the week:

One fun thing I want to do this weekend:

One to-do item I want to accomplish:

One person I want to engage with:

DATE: __/__/__

"It is always the simple that produces the marvelous." —**AMELIA BARR**

One thing that is worrying me today:

One step I can take to address my worry:

One thing I am grateful for today:

One aspiration I have today:

☐ Patience & understanding
☐ Follow-through & accountability
☐ Communicating my feelings
☐ Allowing discomfort
☐ Being vulnerable
☐ Taking a risk
☐ Other:

DATE: __/__/__

"Believe that life is worth living, and your belief will help create the fact." —**WILLIAM JAMES**

One relationship that is unsettled:

One change I can make to improve it:

One beautiful thing I notice:

One happiness I can claim today:

☐ Meditation or prayer
☐ Exercise
☐ Hobby
☐ Act of service
☐ Act of kindness
☐ Being in nature
☐ Other:

"It takes but one positive thought when given a chance to survive and thrive to overpower an entire army of negative thoughts." —**ROBERT H. SCHULLER**

DATE: ___/___/___

One thing I want to get better at:

One step I can take to do that:

One act of kindness I can do today:

One aspiration I have today:

- ☐ Being healthy & active
- ☐ Being caring & considerate
- ☐ Actively engaging with others
- ☐ Being reflective
- ☐ Being quiet
- ☐ Asking for what I need
- ☐ Other:

DATE: __/__/__

"I'm looking forward to influencing others in a positive way. My message is you can do anything if you just put your mind to it." **—JUSTIN BIEBER**

One relationship I am neglecting:

One change I can make to improve it:

One beautiful thing I notice:

One happiness I can claim today:

☐ Meditation or prayer
☐ Exercise
☐ Hobby
☐ Act of service
☐ Act of kindness
☐ Being in nature
☐ Other:

DATE: ___/___/___

"When you have a dream, you've got to grab it and never let go." —**CAROL BURNETT**

One hope I have for the future:

One step I can take toward that goal:

One act of service I can provide today:

One aspiration I have today:

☐ Being slow & deliberate
☐ Being quick & decisive
☐ Listening without judging
☐ Taking action on ideas
☐ Being responsive
☐ Being forgiving
☐ Other:

"The most beautiful thing in the world is, of course, the world itself." —**WALLACE STEVENS**

DATE: ___/___/___

Best encounter of the week:

One fun thing I want to do this weekend:

One to-do item I want to accomplish:

One person I want to engage with:

DATE: __/__/__

"Be brave enough to live life creatively. The creative place where no one else has ever been." —**ALAN ALDA**

One thing that is worrying me today:

One step I can take to address my worry:

One thing I am grateful for today:

One aspiration I have today:

☐ Patience & understanding
☐ Follow-through & accountability
☐ Communicating my feelings
☐ Allowing discomfort
☐ Being vulnerable
☐ Taking a risk
☐ Other:

"In oneself lies the whole world, and if you know how to look and learn, the door is there and the key is in your hand. Nobody on earth can give you either the key or the door to open, except yourself." —**JIDDU KRISHNAMURTI**

DATE: ___/___/___

One relationship that is unsettled:

One change I can make to improve it:

One beautiful thing I notice:

One happiness I can claim today:

☐ Meditation or prayer
☐ Exercise
☐ Hobby
☐ Act of service
☐ Act of kindness
☐ Being in nature
☐ Other:

DATE: __/__/__

"Perpetual optimism is a force multiplier."
—COLIN POWELL

One thing I want to get better at:

One step I can take to do that:

One act of kindness I can
do today:

One aspiration I have today:

☐ Being healthy & active
☐ Being caring & considerate
☐ Actively engaging with
    others
☐ Being reflective
☐ Being quiet
☐ Asking for what I need
☐ Other:

DATE: __/__/__

"Try and be like the turtle—at ease in your own shell." —**BILL COPELAND**

One relationship I am neglecting:

One change I can make to improve it:

One beautiful thing I notice:

One happiness I can claim today:

☐ Meditation or prayer
☐ Exercise
☐ Hobby
☐ Act of service
☐ Act of kindness
☐ Being in nature
☐ Other:

DATE: __/__/__

"I always like to look on the optimistic side of life, but I am realistic enough to know that life is a complex matter." —**WALT DISNEY**

One hope I have for the future:

One step I can take toward that goal:

One act of service I can provide today:

One aspiration I have today:

- ☐ Being slow & deliberate
- ☐ Being quick & decisive
- ☐ Listening without judging
- ☐ Taking action on ideas
- ☐ Being responsive
- ☐ Being forgiving
- ☐ Other:

"The only way to do great work is to love what you do. . . . Don't settle. As with all matters of the heart, you'll know it when you find it."
—STEVE JOBS

DATE: __/__/__

Best encounter of the week:

One fun thing I want to do this weekend:

One to-do item I want to accomplish:

One person I want to engage with:

MONDAY

DATE: __/__/__

"You learn far more from negative leadership than from positive leadership. Because you learn how not to do it. And, therefore, you learn how to do it." **—NORMAN SCHWARZKOPF**

One thing that is worrying
me today:

One step I can take to address
my worry:

One thing I am grateful for today:

One aspiration I have today:

☐ Patience & understanding
☐ Follow-through &
   accountability
☐ Communicating my feelings
☐ Allowing discomfort
☐ Being vulnerable
☐ Taking a risk
☐ Other:

"Find a place inside where there's joy, and the joy will burn out the pain." —**JOSEPH CAMPBELL**

One relationship that is unsettled:

One change I can make to improve it:

One beautiful thing I notice:

One happiness I can claim today:

- ☐ Meditation or prayer
- ☐ Exercise
- ☐ Hobby
- ☐ Act of service
- ☐ Act of kindness
- ☐ Being in nature
- ☐ Other:

DATE: __/__/__

"The rays of happiness, like those of light, are colorless when unbroken."
—HENRY WADSWORTH LONGFELLOW

One thing I want to get better at:

One step I can take to do that:

One act of kindness I can do today:

One aspiration I have today:

- ☐ Being healthy & active
- ☐ Being caring & considerate
- ☐ Actively engaging with others
- ☐ Being reflective
- ☐ Being quiet
- ☐ Asking for what I need
- ☐ Other:

"That's my gift. I let that negativity roll off me like water off a duck's back. If it's not positive, I didn't hear it. If you can overcome that, fights are easy." **—GEORGE FOREMAN**

One relationship I am neglecting:

One change I can make to improve it:

One beautiful thing I notice:

One happiness I can claim today:

- ☐ Meditation or prayer
- ☐ Exercise
- ☐ Hobby
- ☐ Act of service
- ☐ Act of kindness
- ☐ Being in nature
- ☐ Other:

DATE: __/__/__

"The power of imagination makes us infinite."
—**JOHN MUIR**

One hope I have for the future:

One step I can take toward that goal:

One act of service I can provide today:

One aspiration I have today:

- ☐ Being slow & deliberate
- ☐ Being quick & decisive
- ☐ Listening without judging
- ☐ Taking action on ideas
- ☐ Being responsive
- ☐ Being forgiving
- ☐ Other:

*"Redirect the substantial energy of your frustration
and turn it into positive, effective, unstoppable
determination."* **—RALPH MARSTON**

Best encounter of the week:

One fun thing I want to do this
weekend:

One to-do item I want to
accomplish:

One person I want to engage with:

"There is only one way to happiness, and that is to cease worrying about things which are beyond the power of our will." —**EPICTETUS**

DATE: __/__/__

One thing that is worrying me today:

One step I can take to address my worry:

One thing I am grateful for today:

One aspiration I have today:

☐ Patience & understanding
☐ Follow-through & accountability
☐ Communicating my feelings
☐ Allowing discomfort
☐ Being vulnerable
☐ Taking a risk
☐ Other:

DATE: __/__/__

"There is no advertisement as powerful as a positive reputation traveling fast."
—BRIAN KOSLOW

One relationship that is unsettled:

One change I can make to improve it:

One beautiful thing I notice:

One happiness I can claim today:

- ☐ Meditation or prayer
- ☐ Exercise
- ☐ Hobby
- ☐ Act of service
- ☐ Act of kindness
- ☐ Being in nature
- ☐ Other:

"Happiness is not something you postpone for the future; it is something you design for the present."
—JIM ROHN

DATE: __/__/__

One thing I want to get better at:

One step I can take to do that:

One act of kindness I can do today:

One aspiration I have today:

☐ Being healthy & active
☐ Being caring & considerate
☐ Actively engaging with others
☐ Being reflective
☐ Being quiet
☐ Asking for what I need
☐ Other:

DATE: __/__/__

"The learner always begins by finding fault, but the scholar sees the positive merit in everything."
—GEORG WILHELM FRIEDRICH HEGEL

One relationship I am neglecting:

One change I can make to improve it:

One beautiful thing I notice:

One happiness I can claim today:

☐ Meditation or prayer
☐ Exercise
☐ Hobby
☐ Act of service
☐ Act of kindness
☐ Being in nature
☐ Other:

DATE: __/__/__

"From a small seed a mighty trunk may grow."
—AESCHYLUS

One hope I have for the future:

One step I can take toward
that goal:

One act of service I can
provide today:

One aspiration I have today:

- ☐ Being slow & deliberate
- ☐ Being quick & decisive
- ☐ Listening without judging
- ☐ Taking action on ideas
- ☐ Being responsive
- ☐ Being forgiving
- ☐ Other:

DATE: ___/___/___

"So long as you've got your friends about you, and a good positive attitude, you don't really have to care what everyone else thinks." **—GAIL PORTER**

Best encounter of the week:

One fun thing I want to do this weekend:

One to-do item I want to accomplish:

One person I want to engage with:

DATE: ___/___/___

"What we achieve inwardly will change outer reality." —**PLUTARCH**

One thing that is worrying me today:

One step I can take to address my worry:

One thing I am grateful for today:

One aspiration I have today:

☐ Patience & understanding
☐ Follow-through & accountability
☐ Communicating my feelings
☐ Allowing discomfort
☐ Being vulnerable
☐ Taking a risk
☐ Other:

"When someone does something good, applaud! You will make two people happy." —**SAMUEL GOLDWYN**

One relationship that is unsettled:

One change I can make to improve it:

One beautiful thing I notice:

One happiness I can claim today:

☐ Meditation or prayer
☐ Exercise
☐ Hobby
☐ Act of service
☐ Act of kindness
☐ Being in nature
☐ Other:

DATE: __/__/__

"Don't limit yourself. Many people limit themselves to what they think they can do. You can go as far as your mind lets you. What you believe, remember, you can achieve." —**MARY KAY ASH**

One thing I want to get better at:

One step I can take to do that:

One act of kindness I can do today:

One aspiration I have today:

☐ Being healthy & active
☐ Being caring & considerate
☐ Actively engaging with others
☐ Being reflective
☐ Being quiet
☐ Asking for what I need
☐ Other:

"Dream small dreams. If you make them too big, you get overwhelmed and you don't do anything. If you make small goals and accomplish them, it gives you the confidence to go on to higher goals."
—JOHN H. JOHNSON

One relationship I am neglecting:

One change I can make to improve it:

One beautiful thing I notice:

One happiness I can claim today:

☐ Meditation or prayer
☐ Exercise
☐ Hobby
☐ Act of service
☐ Act of kindness
☐ Being in nature
☐ Other:

DATE: __/__/__

"The best way out is always through."
—ROBERT FROST

One hope I have for the future:

One step I can take toward
that goal:

One act of service I can
provide today:

One aspiration I have today:

- ☐ Being slow & deliberate
- ☐ Being quick & decisive
- ☐ Listening without judging
- ☐ Taking action on ideas
- ☐ Being responsive
- ☐ Being forgiving
- ☐ Other:

"I believe in Karma. If the good is sown, the good is collected. When positive things are made, that returns well." **—YANNICK NOAH**

Best encounter of the week:

One fun thing I want to do this weekend:

One to-do item I want to accomplish:

One person I want to engage with:

DATE: __/__/__

"Believe you can and you're halfway there."
—THEODORE ROOSEVELT

One thing that is worrying
me today:

One step I can take to address
my worry:

One thing I am grateful for today:

One aspiration I have today:

- ☐ Patience & understanding
- ☐ Follow-through &
  accountability
- ☐ Communicating my feelings
- ☐ Allowing discomfort
- ☐ Being vulnerable
- ☐ Taking a risk
- ☐ Other:

"Instead of hating, I have chosen to forgive and spend all of my positive energy on changing the world." —**CAMRYN MANHEIM**

DATE: __/__/__

One relationship that is unsettled:

One change I can make to improve it:

One beautiful thing I notice:

One happiness I can claim today:

☐ Meditation or prayer
☐ Exercise
☐ Hobby
☐ Act of service
☐ Act of kindness
☐ Being in nature
☐ Other:

DATE: ___/___/___

"There is nothing impossible to him who will try."
—ATTRIBUTED TO ALEXANDER THE GREAT

One thing I want to get better at:

One step I can take to do that:

One act of kindness I can
do today:

One aspiration I have today:

☐ Being healthy & active
☐ Being caring & considerate
☐ Actively engaging with
 others
☐ Being reflective
☐ Being quiet
☐ Asking for what I need
☐ Other:

DATE: __/__/__

"Pessimism leads to weakness, optimism to power." **—WILLIAM JAMES**

One relationship I am neglecting:

One change I can make to improve it:

One beautiful thing I notice:

One happiness I can claim today:

☐ Meditation or prayer
☐ Exercise
☐ Hobby
☐ Act of service
☐ Act of kindness
☐ Being in nature
☐ Other:

"The only way to discover the limits of the possible is to go beyond them into the impossible."
—ARTHUR C. CLARKE

DATE: ___/___/___

One hope I have for the future:

One step I can take toward that goal:

One act of service I can provide today:

One aspiration I have today:

- ☐ Being slow & deliberate
- ☐ Being quick & decisive
- ☐ Listening without judging
- ☐ Taking action on ideas
- ☐ Being responsive
- ☐ Being forgiving
- ☐ Other:

DATE: ___/___/___

"Positive thinking is more than just a tagline. It changes the way we behave."
—HARVEY MACKAY

Best encounter of the week:

One fun thing I want to do this weekend:

One to-do item I want to accomplish:

One person I want to engage with:

DATE: __/__/__

"Without craftsmanship, inspiration is a mere reed shaken in the wind." —**JOHANNES BRAHMS**

One thing that is worrying me today:

One step I can take to address my worry:

One thing I am grateful for today:

One aspiration I have today:

- ☐ Patience & understanding
- ☐ Follow-through & accountability
- ☐ Communicating my feelings
- ☐ Allowing discomfort
- ☐ Being vulnerable
- ☐ Taking a risk
- ☐ Other:

*"Adopting the right attitude can covert
a negative stress into a positive one."*
—HANS SELYE

One relationship that is unsettled:

One change I can make to
improve it:

One beautiful thing I notice:

One happiness I can claim today:

☐ Meditation or prayer
☐ Exercise
☐ Hobby
☐ Act of service
☐ Act of kindness
☐ Being in nature
☐ Other:

DATE: __/__/__

"Courage, my friends; 'tis not too late to build a better world." —**TOMMY DOUGLAS**

One thing I want to get better at:

One step I can take to do that:

One act of kindness I can do today:

One aspiration I have today:

- ☐ Being healthy & active
- ☐ Being caring & considerate
- ☐ Actively engaging with others
- ☐ Being reflective
- ☐ Being quiet
- ☐ Asking for what I need
- ☐ Other:

DATE: __/__/__

"Even when bad things happen you have to try and use those bad things in a positive manner and really just take the positive out of it."
—NATALIE DU TOIT

One relationship I am neglecting:

One change I can make to improve it:

One beautiful thing I notice:

One happiness I can claim today:

☐ Meditation or prayer
☐ Exercise
☐ Hobby
☐ Act of service
☐ Act of kindness
☐ Being in nature
☐ Other:

DATE: __/__/__

"When deeds speak, words are nothing."
—PIERRE-JOSEPH PROUDHON

One hope I have for the future:

One step I can take toward
that goal:

One act of service I can
provide today:

One aspiration I have today:

- ☐ Being slow & deliberate
- ☐ Being quick & decisive
- ☐ Listening without judging
- ☐ Taking action on ideas
- ☐ Being responsive
- ☐ Being forgiving

"When I learn something new—and it happens every day—I feel a little more at home in this universe, a little more comfortable in the nest."
—BILL MOYERS

Best encounter of the week:

One fun thing I want to do this weekend:

One to-do item I want to accomplish:

1 person I want to engage with:

"Tomorrow is the most important thing in life. Comes into us at midnight very clean. It's perfect when it arrives and it puts itself in our hands. It hopes we've learned something from yesterday." **—JOHN WAYNE**

DATE: ___/___/___

One thing that is worrying me today:

One step I can take to address my worry:

One thing I am grateful for today:

One aspiration I have today:

☐ Patience & understanding
☐ Follow-through & accountability
☐ Communicating my feelings
☐ Allowing discomfort
☐ Being vulnerable
☐ Taking a risk
☐ Other:

DATE: __/__/__

"Look up, laugh loud, talk big, keep the color in your cheek and the fire in your eye, adorn your person, maintain your health, your beauty, and your animal spirits." —**WILLIAM HAZLITT**

One relationship that is unsettled:

One change I can make to improve it:

One beautiful thing I notice:

One happiness I can claim today:

- ☐ Meditation or prayer
- ☐ Exercise
- ☐ Hobby
- ☐ Act of service
- ☐ Act of kindness
- ☐ Being in nature
- ☐ Other:

DATE: ___/___/___

"A lot of times people look at the negative side of what they feel they can't do. I always look on the positive side of what I can do." **—CHUCK NORRIS**

One thing I want to get better at:

One step I can take to do that:

One act of kindness I can do today:

One aspiration I have today:

- ☐ Being healthy & active
- ☐ Being caring & considerate
- ☐ Actively engaging with others
- ☐ Being reflective
- ☐ Being quiet
- ☐ Asking for what I need
- ☐ Other:

"Thought is the wind, knowledge the sail, and mankind the vessel." **—AUGUSTUS HARE**

One relationship I am neglecting:

One change I can make to improve it:

One beautiful thing I notice:

One happiness I can claim today:

☐ Meditation or prayer
☐ Exercise
☐ Hobby
☐ Act of service
☐ Act of kindness
☐ Being in nature
☐ Other:

DATE: __/__/__

"The gift of fantasy has meant more to me than my talent for absorbing positive knowledge."
—ALBERT EINSTEIN

One hope I have for the future:

One step I can take toward that goal:

One act of service I can provide today:

One aspiration I have today:

☐ Being slow & deliberate
☐ Being quick & decisive
☐ Listening without judging
☐ Taking action on ideas
☐ Being responsive
☐ Being forgiving
☐ Other:

A TIME TO REVIEW

DATE: __/__/__

| What have I accomplished? | What has changed about me? |

| What have I gotten better at? | What person have I gotten closer to? |

"If the message is positive, it can make your day a little better." **—YAO MING**

DATE: ___/___/___

One thing that is worrying me today:

One step I can take to address my worry:

One thing I am grateful for today:

One aspiration I have today:

☐ Patience & understanding
☐ Follow-through & accountability
☐ Communicating my feelings
☐ Allowing discomfort
☐ Being vulnerable
☐ Taking a risk

"There is nothing stronger in the world than gentleness." —HAN SUYIN

DATE: __/__/__

One relationship that is unsettled:

One change I can make to improve it:

One beautiful thing I notice:

One happiness I can claim today:

☐ Meditation or prayer
☐ Exercise
☐ Hobby
☐ Act of service
☐ Act of kindness
☐ Being in nature
☐ Other:

DATE: __/__/__

"The way positive reinforcement is carried out is more important than the amount."
—B. F. SKINNER

One thing I want to get better at:

One step I can take to do that:

One act of kindness I can do today:

One aspiration I have today:

- ☐ Being healthy & active
- ☐ Being caring & considerate
- ☐ Actively engaging with others
- ☐ Being reflective
- ☐ Being quiet
- ☐ Asking for what I need
- ☐ Other:

"*God sleeps in the minerals, awakens in the plants,
 walks in the animals, and thinks in man.*"
—ARTHUR YOUNG

One relationship I am neglecting:

One change I can make to improve it:

One beautiful thing I notice:

One happiness I can claim today:

☐ Meditation or prayer
☐ Exercise
☐ Hobby
☐ Act of service
☐ Act of kindness
☐ Being in nature
☐ Other:

DATE: __/__/__

"I was blessed with certain gifts and talents and God gave them to me to be the best person I can be and to have a positive impact on other people."
—**BRYAN CLAY**

One hope I have for the future:

One step I can take toward that goal:

One act of service I can provide today:

One aspiration I have today:

- ☐ Being slow & deliberate
- ☐ Being quick & decisive
- ☐ Listening without judging
- ☐ Taking action on ideas
- ☐ Being responsive
- ☐ Being forgiving
- ☐ Other:

DATE: __/__/__

"It is in your moments of decision that your destiny is shaped." —**TONY ROBBINS**

Best encounter of the week:

One fun thing I want to do this weekend:

One to-do item I want to accomplish:

One person I want to engage with:

DATE: ___/___/___

"There are powers inside of you which, if you could discover and use, would make of you everything you ever dreamed or imagined you could become."
—ORISON SWETT MARDEN

One thing that is worrying me today:

One step I can take to address my worry:

One thing I am grateful for today:

One aspiration I have today:

- ☐ Patience & understanding
- ☐ Follow-through & accountability
- ☐ Communicating my feelings
- ☐ Allowing discomfort
- ☐ Being vulnerable
- ☐ Taking a risk
- ☐ Other:

DATE: __/__/__

"As we express our gratitude, we must never forget that the highest appreciation is not to utter words, but to live by them." **—JOHN F. KENNEDY**

One relationship that is unsettled:

One change I can make to improve it:

One beautiful thing I notice:

One happiness I can claim today:

- ☐ Meditation or prayer
- ☐ Exercise
- ☐ Hobby
- ☐ Act of service
- ☐ Act of kindness
- ☐ Being in nature
- ☐ Other:

"Chaotic people often have chaotic lives, and I think they create that. But if you try and have an inner peace and a positive attitude, I think you attract that." —IMELDA STAUNTON

One thing I want to get better at:

One step I can take to do that:

One act of kindness I can do today:

One aspiration I have today:

☐ Being healthy & active
☐ Being caring & considerate
☐ Actively engaging with others
☐ Being reflective
☐ Being quiet
☐ Asking for what I need
☐ Other:

"As knowledge increases, wonder deepens."
—CHARLES MORGAN

One relationship I am neglecting:

One change I can make to improve it:

One beautiful thing I notice:

One happiness I can claim today:

☐ Meditation or prayer
☐ Exercise
☐ Hobby
☐ Act of service
☐ Act of kindness
☐ Being in nature
☐ Other:

DATE: __/__/__

"The things that we love tell us what we are." —THOMAS AQUINAS

One hope I have for the future:

One step I can take toward that goal:

One act of service I can provide today:

One aspiration I have today:

☐ Being slow & deliberate
☐ Being quick & decisive
☐ Listening without judging
☐ Taking action on ideas
☐ Being responsive
☐ Being forgiving
☐ Other:

"You can't make positive choices for the rest of your life without an environment that makes those choices easy, natural, and enjoyable."
—DEEPAK CHOPRA

Best encounter of the week:

One fun thing I want to do this weekend:

One to-do item I want to accomplish:

One person I want to engage with:

DATE: __/__/__

"Thinking: the talking of the soul with itself." —**PLATO**

One thing that is worrying me today:

One step I can take to address my worry:

One thing I am grateful for today:

One aspiration I have today:

- ☐ Patience & understanding
- ☐ Follow-through & accountability
- ☐ Communicating my feelings
- ☐ Allowing discomfort
- ☐ Being vulnerable
- ☐ Taking a risk
- ☐ Other:

*"Winners make a habit of manufacturing their
own positive expectations in advance of the event."*
—BRIAN TRACY

DATE: ___/___/___

One relationship that is unsettled:

One change I can make to
improve it:

One beautiful thing I notice:

One happiness I can claim today:

- ☐ Meditation or prayer
- ☐ Exercise
- ☐ Hobby
- ☐ Act of service
- ☐ Act of kindness
- ☐ Being in nature
- ☐ Other:

DATE: __/__/__

"It is not ignorance but knowledge which is the mother of wonder." —**JOSEPH WOOD KRUTCH**

One thing I want to get better at:

One step I can take to do that:

One act of kindness I can do today:

One aspiration I have today:

- ☐ Being healthy & active
- ☐ Being caring & considerate
- ☐ Actively engaging with others
- ☐ Being reflective
- ☐ Being quiet
- ☐ Asking for what I need
- ☐ Other:

"I believe that you should gravitate to people who are doing productive and positive things with their lives." **—NADIA COMANECI**

DATE: __/__/__

One relationship I am neglecting:

One change I can make to improve it:

One beautiful thing I notice:

One happiness I can claim today:

☐ Meditation or prayer
☐ Exercise
☐ Hobby
☐ Act of service
☐ Act of kindness
☐ Being in nature
☐ Other:

DATE: ___/___/___

"Your destiny is to fulfill those things upon which you focus most intently. . . . Your life is always moving toward something." —**RALPH MARSTON**

One hope I have for the future:

One step I can take toward that goal:

One act of service I can provide today:

One aspiration I have today:

☐ Being slow & deliberate
☐ Being quick & decisive
☐ Listening without judging
☐ Taking action on ideas
☐ Being responsive
☐ Being forgiving
☐ Other:

"*A single sunbeam is enough to drive away many shadows.*" —**FRANCIS OF ASSISI**

Best encounter of the week:

One fun thing I want to do this weekend:

One to-do item I want to accomplish:

One person I want to engage with:

DATE: ___/___/___

"I don't want to waste anyone's time or money. I want to give people some truth and positive heart lift." **—YASLIN BEY**

One thing that is worrying me today:

One step I can take to address my worry:

One thing I am grateful for today:

One aspiration I have today:

☐ Patience & understanding
☐ Follow-through & accountability
☐ Communicating my feelings
☐ Allowing discomfort
☐ Being vulnerable
☐ Taking a risk

DATE: ___/___/___

"How wonderful it is that nobody need wait a single moment before starting to improve the world." —**ANNE FRANK**

One relationship that is unsettled:

One change I can make to improve it:

One beautiful thing I notice:

One happiness I can claim today:

☐ Meditation or prayer
☐ Exercise
☐ Hobby
☐ Act of service
☐ Act of kindness
☐ Being in nature
☐ Other:

"Some people never contribute anything positive to society; they may even drain our resources, but most of us try to do something better, to give back."
—MARTIN YAN

One thing I want to get better at:

One step I can take to do that:

One act of kindness I can do today:

One aspiration I have today:

- ☐ Being healthy & active
- ☐ Being caring & considerate
- ☐ Actively engaging with others
- ☐ Being reflective
- ☐ Being quiet
- ☐ Asking for what I need
- ☐ Other:

"Man never made any material as resilient as the human spirit." —**BERNARD WILLIAMS**

DATE: ___/___/___

One relationship I am neglecting:

One change I can make to improve it:

One beautiful thing I notice:

One happiness I can claim today:

☐ Meditation or prayer
☐ Exercise
☐ Hobby
☐ Act of service
☐ Act of kindness
☐ Being in nature
☐ Other:

DATE: __/__/__

"In a gentle way, you can shake the world."
—MAHATMA GANDHI

One hope I have for the future:

One step I can take toward that goal:

One act of service I can provide today:

One aspiration I have today:

☐ Being slow & deliberate
☐ Being quick & decisive
☐ Listening without judging
☐ Taking action on ideas
☐ Being responsive
☐ Being forgiving
☐ Other:

"Why be negative when you can enjoy life and be positive? That's something I learned over the years." **—VIRGIL VAN DIJK**

Best encounter of the week:

One fun thing I want to do this weekend:

One to-do item I want to accomplish:

One person I want to engage with:

DATE: __/__/__

*"Too low they build, who build
beneath the stars."* —**EDWARD YOUNG**

One thing that is worrying
me today:

One step I can take to address
my worry:

One thing I am grateful for today:

One aspiration I have today:

- [ ] Patience & understanding
- [ ] Follow-through &
  accountability
- [ ] Communicating my feelings
- [ ] Allowing discomfort
- [ ] Being vulnerable
- [ ] Taking a risk
- [ ] Other:

DATE: __/__/__

"There is a sense that things, if you keep positive and optimistic about what can be done, do work out."
—HILLARY CLINTON

One relationship that is unsettled:

One change I can make to improve it:

One beautiful thing I notice:

One happiness I can claim today:

☐ Meditation or prayer
☐ Exercise
☐ Hobby
☐ Act of service
☐ Act of kindness
☐ Being in nature
☐ Other:

DATE: __/__/__

"A place for everything, everything in its place."
—ANONYMOUS

One thing I want to get better at:

One step I can take to do that:

One act of kindness I can do today:

One aspiration I have today:

☐ Being healthy & active
☐ Being caring & considerate
☐ Actively engaging with others
☐ Being reflective
☐ Being quiet
☐ Asking for what I need
☐ Other:

"So there was a fire inside me. And that fire inside you, it can be turned into a negative form or a positive form. And I gradually realized that I had this fire and it had to be used in a positive way."
—JOHN NEWCOMBE

One relationship I am neglecting:

One change I can make to improve it:

One beautiful thing I notice:

One happiness I can claim today:

- ☐ Meditation or prayer
- ☐ Exercise
- ☐ Hobby
- ☐ Act of service
- ☐ Act of kindness
- ☐ Being in nature
- ☐ Other:

*"Whatever you vividly imagine, ardently desire,
sincerely believe, and enthusiastically act upon
must inevitably come to pass"* —**PAUL J. MEYER**

One hope I have for the future:

One step I can take toward
that goal:

One act of service I can
provide today:

One aspiration I have today:

☐ Being slow & deliberate
☐ Being quick & decisive
☐ Listening without judging
☐ Taking action on ideas
☐ Being responsive
☐ Being forgiving
☐ Other:

"Wondrous is the strength of cheerfulness, and its power of endurance—the cheerful man will do more in the same time, will do it better, will preserve it longer, than the sad or sullen."
—THOMAS CARLYLE

Best encounter of the week:

One fun thing I want to do this weekend:

One to-do item I want to accomplish:

One person I want to engage with:

"Find out who you are and be that person. That's what your soul was put on this earth to be. Find that truth, live that truth and everything else will come." —**ELLEN DEGENERES**

DATE: __/__/__

One thing that is worrying me today:

One step I can take to address my worry:

One thing I am grateful for today:

One aspiration I have today:

☐ Patience & understanding
☐ Follow-through & accountability
☐ Communicating my feelings
☐ Allowing discomfort
☐ Being vulnerable
☐ Taking a risk
☐ Other:

"We have a duty to show up in the world with meaning and purpose and commitment to doing good." —**MEENA HARRIS**

DATE: __/__/__

One relationship that is unsettled:

One change I can make to improve it:

One beautiful thing I notice:

One happiness I can claim today:

- ☐ Meditation or prayer
- ☐ Exercise
- ☐ Hobby
- ☐ Act of service
- ☐ Act of kindness
- ☐ Being in nature
- ☐ Other:

"I believe that one defines oneself by reinvention. To not be like your parents. To not be like your friends. To be yourself. To cut yourself out of stone."
—HENRY ROLLINS

DATE: __/__/__

One thing I want to get better at:

One step I can take to do that:

One act of kindness I can do today:

One aspiration I have today:

☐ Being healthy & active
☐ Being caring & considerate
☐ Actively engaging with others
☐ Being reflective
☐ Being quiet
☐ Asking for what I need
☐ Other:

"Excellence encourages one about life generally; it shows the spiritual wealth of the world."
—GEORGE ELIOT

DATE: __/__/__

One relationship I am neglecting:

One change I can make to improve it:

One beautiful thing I notice:

One happiness I can claim today:

☐ Meditation or prayer
☐ Exercise
☐ Hobby
☐ Act of service
☐ Act of kindness
☐ Being in nature
☐ Other:

DATE: __/__/__

"*I believe there's an inner power that makes winners or losers. And the winners are those ones who really listen to the truth of their hearts.*"
—SYLVESTER STALLONE

One hope I have for the future:

One step I can take toward that goal:

One act of service I can provide today:

One aspiration I have today:

- ☐ Being slow & deliberate
- ☐ Being quick & decisive
- ☐ Listening without judging
- ☐ Taking action on ideas
- ☐ Being responsive
- ☐ Being forgiving

"*There is only one thing for us to do, and that is to do our level best right where we are every day of our lives; to use our best judgment, and then to trust the rest to that Power which holds the forces of the universe in his hands.*"
—ORISON SWETT MARDEN

Best encounter of the week:

One fun thing I want to do this weekend:

One to-do item I want to accomplish:

One person I want to engage with:

DATE: __/__/__

"*Hope is some extraordinary spiritual grace that
God gives us to control our fears, not to oust them.*"
—VINCENT MCNABB

One thing that is worrying
me today:

One step I can take to address
my worry:

One thing I am grateful for today:

One aspiration I have today:

☐ Patience & understanding
☐ Follow-through &
accountability
☐ Communicating my feelings
☐ Allowing discomfort
☐ Being vulnerable
☐ Taking a risk
☐ Other:

DATE: ___/___/___

"A mediocre idea that generates enthusiasm will go further than a great idea that inspires no one."
—MARY KAY ASH

One relationship that is unsettled:

One change I can make to improve it:

One beautiful thing I notice:

One happiness I can claim today:

☐ Meditation or prayer
☐ Exercise
☐ Hobby
☐ Act of service
☐ Act of kindness
☐ Being in nature
☐ Other:

"I've been absolutely terrified every moment of my life—and I've never let it keep me from doing a single thing I wanted to do."
—GEORGIA O'KEEFFE

One thing I want to get better at:

One step I can take to do that:

One act of kindness I can do today:

One aspiration I have today:

☐ Being healthy & active
☐ Being caring & considerate
☐ Actively engaging with others
☐ Being reflective
☐ Being quiet
☐ Asking for what I need
☐ Other:

"Satisfaction consists in freedom from pain, which is the positive element of life."
—ARTHUR SCHOPENHAUER

One relationship I am neglecting:

One change I can make to improve it:

One beautiful thing I notice:

One happiness I can claim today:

☐ Meditation or prayer
☐ Exercise
☐ Hobby
☐ Act of service
☐ Act of kindness
☐ Being in nature
☐ Other:

DATE: __/__/__

"Shoot for the moon and if you miss you will still be among the stars." —**LES BROWN**

One hope I have for the future:

One step I can take toward that goal:

One act of service I can provide today:

One aspiration I have today:

☐ Being slow & deliberate
☐ Being quick & decisive
☐ Listening without judging
☐ Taking action on ideas
☐ Being responsive
☐ Being forgiving
☐ Other:

"A year or so ago I went through all the people in my life and asked myself: does this person inspire me, genuinely love me, and support me unconditionally? I wanted nothing but positive influences in my life." —**MENA SUVARI**

Best encounter of the week:

One fun thing I want to do this weekend:

One to-do item I want to accomplish:

One person I want to engage with:

DATE: ___/___/___

"A #2 pencil and a dream can take you anywhere." **—JOYCE MEYER**

One thing that is worrying me today:

One step I can take to address my worry:

One thing I am grateful for today:

One aspiration I have today:

☐ Patience & understanding
☐ Follow-through & accountability
☐ Communicating my feelings
☐ Allowing discomfort
☐ Being vulnerable
☐ Taking a risk
☐ Other:

> *"Like success, failure is many things to many people. With a positive mental attitude, failure is a learning experience, a rung on the ladder, a plateau at which you get your thoughts in order and prepare to try again."*
> —**W. CLEMENT STONE**

One relationship that is unsettled:

One change I can make to improve it:

One beautiful thing I notice:

One happiness I can claim today:

- ☐ Meditation or prayer
- ☐ Exercise
- ☐ Hobby
- ☐ Act of service
- ☐ Act of kindness
- ☐ Being in nature
- ☐ Other:

DATE: ___/___/___

"I believe that if one always looked at the skies,
one would end up with wings."
—GUSTAVE FLAUBERT

One thing I want to get better at:

One step I can take to do that:

One act of kindness I can
do today:

One aspiration I have today:

☐ Being healthy & active
☐ Being caring & considerate
☐ Actively engaging with
    others
☐ Being reflective
☐ Being quiet
☐ Asking for what I need
☐ Other

"If it's great stuff, the people who consume it are nourished. It's a positive force." —**MANUEL PUIG**

One relationship I am neglecting:

One change I can make to improve it:

One beautiful thing I notice:

One happiness I can claim today:

- ☐ Meditation or prayer
- ☐ Exercise
- ☐ Hobby
- ☐ Act of service
- ☐ Act of kindness
- ☐ Being in nature
- ☐ Other:

"Of all things visible, the highest is the heaven of the fixed stars." **—NICOLAUS COPERNICUS**

DATE: ___/___/___

One hope I have for the future:

One step I can take toward that goal:

One act of service I can provide today:

One aspiration I have today:

- ☐ Being slow & deliberate
- ☐ Being quick & decisive
- ☐ Listening without judging
- ☐ Taking action on ideas
- ☐ Being responsive
- ☐ Being forgiving
- ☐ Other:

"Every moment and every event of every man's life on earth plants something in his soul." —**THOMAS MERTON**

Best encounter of the week:

One fun thing I want to do this weekend:

One to-do item I want to accomplish:

One person I want to engage with:

DATE: ___/___/___

"A positive attitude can really make dreams come true—it did for me." **–DAVID BAILEY**

One thing that is worrying me today:

One step I can take to address my worry:

One thing I am grateful for today:

One aspiration I have today:

- ☐ Patience & understanding
- ☐ Follow-through & accountability
- ☐ Communicating my feelings
- ☐ Allowing discomfort
- ☐ Being vulnerable
- ☐ Taking a risk
- ☐ Other:

"Health is the greatest gift, contentment the greatest wealth, faithfulness the best relationship."
—BUDDHA

DATE: __/__/__

One relationship that is unsettled:

One change I can make to improve it:

One beautiful thing I notice:

One happiness I can claim today:

☐ Meditation or prayer
☐ Exercise
☐ Hobby
☐ Act of service
☐ Act of kindness
☐ Being in nature
☐ Other:

DATE: __/__/__

"Don't forget to tell yourself positive things daily! You must love yourself internally to glow externally." —**HANNAH BRONFMAN**

One thing I want to get better at:

One step I can take to do that:

One act of kindness I can do today:

One aspiration I have today:

☐ Being healthy & active
☐ Being caring & considerate
☐ Actively engaging with others
☐ Being reflective
☐ Being quiet
☐ Asking for what I need
☐ Other:

DATE: __/__/__

"The undertaking of a new action brings new strength." —**RICHARD L. EVANS**

One relationship I am neglecting:

One change I can make to improve it:

One beautiful thing I notice:

One happiness I can claim today:

- ☐ Meditation or prayer
- ☐ Exercise
- ☐ Hobby
- ☐ Act of service
- ☐ Act of kindness
- ☐ Being in nature
- ☐ Other:

DATE: __/__/__

"In times of great stress or adversity, it's always best to keep busy, to plow your anger and your energy into something positive." **—LEE IACOCCA**

One hope I have for the future:

One step I can take toward that goal:

One act of service I can provide today:

One aspiration I have today:

- ☐ Being slow & deliberate
- ☐ Being quick & decisive
- ☐ Listening without judging
- ☐ Taking action on ideas
- ☐ Being responsive
- ☐ Being forgiving
- ☐ Other:

DATE: __/__/__

*"I am an acme of things accomplish'd,
and I an encloser of things to be."*
—WALT WHITMAN

Best encounter of the week:

One fun thing I want to do this weekend:

One to-do item I want to accomplish:

One person I want to engage with:

DATE: __/__/__

"Successful people maintain a positive focus in life no matter what is going on around them."
—JACK CANFIELD

One thing that is worrying me today:

One step I can take to address my worry:

One thing I am grateful for today:

One aspiration I have today:

☐ Patience & understanding
☐ Follow-through & accountability
☐ Communicating my feelings
☐ Allowing discomfort
☐ Being vulnerable
☐ Taking a risk
☐ Other:

One relationship that is unsettled:

One change I can make to improve it:

One beautiful thing I notice:

One happiness I can claim today:

- ☐ Meditation or prayer
- ☐ Exercise
- ☐ Hobby
- ☐ Act of service
- ☐ Act of kindness
- ☐ Being in nature
- ☐ Other:

"Your positive action combined with positive thinking results in success." —**SHIV KHERA**

DATE: __/__/__

One thing I want to get better at:

One step I can take to do that:

One act of kindness I can do today:

One aspiration I have today:

- ☐ Being healthy & active
- ☐ Being caring & considerate
- ☐ Actively engaging with others
- ☐ Being reflective
- ☐ Being quiet
- ☐ Asking for what I need
- ☐ Other:

DATE: __/__/__

"The limits of the possible can only be defined by going beyond them into the impossible."
—ARTHUR C. CLARKE

One relationship I am neglecting:

One change I can make to improve it:

One beautiful thing I notice:

One happiness I can claim today:

- ☐ Meditation or prayer
- ☐ Exercise
- ☐ Hobby
- ☐ Act of service
- ☐ Act of kindness
- ☐ Being in nature
- ☐ Other:

"Stay positive and happy. Work hard and don't give up. Be open to criticism and keep learning. Surround yourself with happy, warm, and genuine people." —**TENA DESAE**

DATE: ___/___/___

One hope I have for the future:

One step I can take toward that goal:

One act of service I can provide today:

One aspiration I have today:

☐ Being slow & deliberate
☐ Being quick & decisive
☐ Listening without judging
☐ Taking action on ideas
☐ Being responsive
☐ Being forgiving
☐ Other:

"*Throw your dreams into space like a kite, and you do not know what it will bring back, a new life, a new friend, a new love, a new country.*"
—**ANAÏS NIN**

Best encounter of the week:

One fun thing I want to do this weekend:

One to-do item I want to accomplish:

One person I want to engage with:

DATE: ___/___/___

"Love yourself. It is important to stay positive because beauty comes from the inside out."
—JENN PROSKE

One thing that is worrying me today:

One step I can take to address my worry:

One thing I am grateful for today:

One aspiration I have today:

- ☐ Patience & understanding
- ☐ Follow-through & accountability
- ☐ Communicating my feelings
- ☐ Allowing discomfort
- ☐ Being vulnerable
- ☐ Taking a risk
- ☐ Other:

DATE: __/__/__

"Let your life lightly dance on the edges of Time like dew on the tip of a leaf."
—RABINDRANATH TAGORE

One relationship that is unsettled:

One change I can make to improve it:

One beautiful thing I notice:

One happiness I can claim today:

- [ ] Meditation or prayer
- [ ] Exercise
- [ ] Hobby
- [ ] Act of service
- [ ] Act of kindness
- [ ] Being in nature
- [ ] Other:

"Choosing to be positive and having a grateful attitude is going to determine how you're going to live your life." **—JOEL OSTEEN**

DATE: __/__/__

One thing I want to get better at:

One step I can take to do that:

One act of kindness I can do today:

One aspiration I have today:

☐ Being healthy & active
☐ Being caring & considerate
☐ Actively engaging with others
☐ Being reflective
☐ Being quiet
☐ Asking for what I need
☐ Other:

DATE: ___/___/___

"Memories of our lives, of our works, and our deeds will continue in others." **—ROSA PARKS**

One relationship I am neglecting:

One change I can make to improve it:

One beautiful thing I notice:

One happiness I can claim today:

☐ Meditation or prayer
☐ Exercise
☐ Hobby
☐ Act of service
☐ Act of kindness
☐ Being in nature
☐ Other:

DATE: ___/___/___

"*At the end of the day, the most overwhelming key to a child's success is the positive involvement of parents.*" —**JANE D. HULL**

One hope I have for the future:

One step I can take toward that goal:

One act of service I can provide today:

One aspiration I have today:

☐ Being slow & deliberate
☐ Being quick & decisive
☐ Listening without judging
☐ Taking action on ideas
☐ Being responsive
☐ Being forgiving
☐ Other:

"A lot of things are going to happen that you can't necessarily control all the time, but you can control what you do after it happens." —**LONZO BALL**

WEEKEND

DATE: ___/___/___

Best encounter of the week:

One fun thing I want to do this weekend:

One to-do item I want to accomplish:

One person I want to engage with:

DATE: __/__/__

*"Every day we should hear at least one little song,
read one good poem, see one exquisite picture, and
if possible, speak a few sensible words."*
—JOHANN WOLFGANG VON GOETHE

One thing that is worrying
me today:

One step I can take to address
my worry:

One thing I am grateful for today:

One aspiration I have today:

- ☐ Patience & understanding
- ☐ Follow-through &
  accountability
- ☐ Communicating my feelings
- ☐ Allowing discomfort
- ☐ Being vulnerable
- ☐ Taking a risk
- ☐ Other:

*"Stop saying negative things about yourself.
Look in the mirror and find something about
yourself that's positive and celebrate that!"*
—TYRA BANKS

DATE: __/__/__

One relationship that is unsettled:

One change I can make to improve it:

One beautiful thing I notice:

One happiness I can claim today:

☐ Meditation or prayer
☐ Exercise
☐ Hobby
☐ Act of service
☐ Act of kindness
☐ Being in nature
☐ Other:

"Follow your bliss and the universe will open doors where there were only walls."
—JOSEPH CAMPBELL

DATE: __/__/__

One thing I want to get better at:

One step I can take to do that:

One act of kindness I can do today:

One aspiration I have today:

- ☐ Being healthy & active
- ☐ Being caring & considerate
- ☐ Actively engaging with others
- ☐ Being reflective
- ☐ Being quiet
- ☐ Asking for what I need
- ☐ Other:

DATE: __/__/__

"You change your life by changing your heart." —**MAX LUCADO**

One relationship I am neglecting:

One change I can make to improve it:

One beautiful thing I notice:

One happiness I can claim today:

- ☐ Meditation or prayer
- ☐ Exercise
- ☐ Hobby
- ☐ Act of service
- ☐ Act of kindness
- ☐ Being in nature
- ☐ Other:

DATE: __/__/__

"I surround myself with good people who make me feel great and give me positive energy."
—**ALI KRIEGER**

One hope I have for the future:

One step I can take toward that goal:

One act of service I can provide today:

One aspiration I have today:

☐ Being slow & deliberate
☐ Being quick & decisive
☐ Listening without judging
☐ Taking action on ideas
☐ Being responsive
☐ Being forgiving
☐ Other:

"Every moment of one's life is meditation."
—BUDDHA

Best encounter of the week:

One fun thing I want to do this weekend:

One to-do item I want to accomplish:

One person I want to engage with:

"While you're going through this process of trying to find the satisfaction in your work, pretend you feel satisfied. If you act like you're having fun, you'll find you are having fun."
—JEAN CHATZKY

DATE: ___/___/___

One thing that is worrying me today:

One step I can take to address my worry:

One thing I am grateful for today:

One aspiration I have today:

☐ Patience & understanding
☐ Follow-through & accountability
☐ Communicating my feelings
☐ Allowing discomfort
☐ Being vulnerable
☐ Taking a risk
☐ Other:

DATE: __/__/__

"When the sun is shining I can do anything; no mountain is too high, no trouble too difficult to overcome." —**WILMA RUDOLPH**

One relationship that is unsettled:

One change I can make to improve it:

One beautiful thing I notice:

One happiness I can claim today:

☐ Meditation or prayer
☐ Exercise
☐ Hobby
☐ Act of service
☐ Act of kindness
☐ Being in nature
☐ Other:

"Inspiration comes from within yourself. One has to be positive. When you're positive, good things happen." —**DEEP ROY**

DATE: __/__/__

One thing I want to get better at:

One step I can take to do that:

One act of kindness I can do today:

One aspiration I have today:

- ☐ Being healthy & active
- ☐ Being caring & considerate
- ☐ Actively engaging with others
- ☐ Being reflective
- ☐ Being quiet
- ☐ Asking for what I need
- ☐ Other:

DATE: __/__/__

"It is only in sorrow bad weather masters us; in joy we face the storm and defy it." —**AMELIA BARR**

One relationship I am neglecting:

One change I can make to improve it:

One beautiful thing I notice:

One happiness I can claim today:

☐ Meditation or prayer
☐ Exercise
☐ Hobby
☐ Act of service
☐ Act of kindness
☐ Being in nature
☐ Other:

"A hero is someone who has given his or her life to something bigger than oneself."
—JOSEPH CAMPBELL

DATE: __/__/__

One hope I have for the future:

One step I can take toward that goal:

One act of service I can provide today:

One aspiration I have today:

☐ Being slow & deliberate
☐ Being quick & decisive
☐ Listening without judging
☐ Taking action on ideas
☐ Being responsive
☐ Being forgiving
☐ Other:

A TIME TO REVIEW

DATE: __/__/__

What have I accomplished?

What has changed about me?

What have I gotten better at?

What person have I gotten closer to?

DATE: __/__/__

"What you feel inside reflects on your face. So be happy and positive all the time." **—SRIDEVI**

One thing that is worrying me today:

One step I can take to address my worry:

One thing I am grateful for today:

One aspiration I have today:

☐ Patience & understanding
☐ Follow-through & accountability
☐ Communicating my feelings
☐ Allowing discomfort
☐ Being vulnerable
☐ Taking a risk
☐ Other:

DATE: ___/___/___

"All you need is the plan, the road map, and the courage to press on to your destination."
—EARL NIGHTINGALE

One relationship that is unsettled:

One change I can make to improve it:

One beautiful thing I notice:

One happiness I can claim today:

- ☐ Meditation or prayer
- ☐ Exercise
- ☐ Hobby
- ☐ Act of service
- ☐ Act of kindness
- ☐ Being in nature
- ☐ Other:

"A positive attitude causes a chain reaction of positive thoughts, events, and outcomes. It is a catalyst and it sparks extraordinary results." —**WADE BOGGS**

One thing I want to get better at:

One step I can take to do that:

One act of kindness I can do today:

One aspiration I have today:

☐ Being healthy & active
☐ Being caring & considerate
☐ Actively engaging with others
☐ Being reflective
☐ Being quiet
☐ Asking for what I need
☐ Other:

DATE: __/__/__

"Joy descends gently upon us like the evening dew and does not patter down like a hailstorm."
—JEAN PAUL

One relationship I am neglecting:

One change I can make to improve it:

One beautiful thing I notice:

One happiness I can claim today:

☐ Meditation or prayer
☐ Exercise
☐ Hobby
☐ Act of service
☐ Act of kindness
☐ Being in nature
☐ Other:

DATE: __/__/__

"It doesn't matter what cards you're dealt. It's what you do with those cards. Never complain. Just keep pushing forward. Find a positive in anything and just fight for it." —**BAKER MAYFIELD**

One hope I have for the future:

One step I can take toward that goal:

One act of service I can provide today:

One aspiration I have today:

- ☐ Being slow & deliberate
- ☐ Being quick & decisive
- ☐ Listening without judging
- ☐ Taking action on ideas
- ☐ Being responsive
- ☐ Being forgiving
- ☐ Other:

*"Love the moment, and the energy of that moment
will spread beyond all boundaries."*
—CORITA KENT

DATE: __/__/__

Best encounter of the week:

One fun thing I want to do this weekend:

One to-do item I want to accomplish:

One person I want to engage with:

"I believe that happy girls are the prettiest girls."
—AUDREY HEPBURN

DATE: ___/___/___

One thing that is worrying
me today:

One step I can take to address
my worry:

One thing I am grateful for today:

One aspiration I have today:

☐ Patience & understanding
☐ Follow-through &
   accountability
☐ Communicating my feelings
☐ Allowing discomfort
☐ Being vulnerable
☐ Taking a risk
☐ Other:

"Having a positive mental attitude is asking how something can be done rather than saying it can't be done." —**BO BENNETT**

DATE: __/__/__

One relationship that is unsettled:

One change I can make to improve it:

One beautiful thing I notice:

One happiness I can claim today:

- ☐ Meditation or prayer
- ☐ Exercise
- ☐ Hobby
- ☐ Act of service
- ☐ Act of kindness
- ☐ Being in nature
- ☐ Other:

DATE: ___/___/___

"Reach for it. Push yourself as far as you can."
—CHRISTA MCAULIFFE

One thing I want to get better at:

One step I can take to do that:

One act of kindness I can do today:

One aspiration I have today:

☐ Being healthy & active
☐ Being caring & considerate
☐ Actively engaging with others
☐ Being reflective
☐ Being quiet
☐ Asking for what I need
☐ Other:

"A strong positive mental attitude will create more miracles than any wonder drug."
—PATRICIA NEAL

One relationship I am neglecting:

One change I can make to improve it:

One beautiful thing I notice:

One happiness I can claim today:

- ☐ Meditation or prayer
- ☐ Exercise
- ☐ Hobby
- ☐ Act of service
- ☐ Act of kindness
- ☐ Being in nature
- ☐ Other:

"The more you are positive and say, 'I want to have a good life,' the more you build that reality for yourself by creating the life that you want."
—CHRIS PINE

One hope I have for the future:

One step I can take toward that goal:

One act of service I can provide today:

One aspiration I have today:

☐ Being slow & deliberate
☐ Being quick & decisive
☐ Listening without judging
☐ Taking action on ideas
☐ Being responsive
☐ Being forgiving
☐ Other:

DATE: __/__/__

"A compliment is something like a kiss through a veil." —**VICTOR HUGO**

Best encounter of the week:

One fun thing I want to do this weekend:

One to-do item I want to accomplish:

One person I want to engage with:

"For myself I am an optimist—it does not seem to be much use being anything else."
—WINSTON CHURCHILL

DATE: __/__/__

One thing that is worrying
me today:

One step I can take to address
my worry:

One thing I am grateful for today:

One aspiration I have today:

- ☐ Patience & understanding
- ☐ Follow-through & accountability
- ☐ Communicating my feelings
- ☐ Allowing discomfort
- ☐ Being vulnerable
- ☐ Taking a risk
- ☐ Other:

"The bird is powered by its own life and by its motivation." —**A. P. J. ABDUL KALAM**

DATE: __/__/__

One relationship that is unsettled:

One change I can make to improve it:

One beautiful thing I notice:

One happiness I can claim today:

☐ Meditation or prayer
☐ Exercise
☐ Hobby
☐ Act of service
☐ Act of kindness
☐ Being in nature
☐ Other:

"In every day, there are 1,440 minutes. That means we have 1,440 daily opportunities to make a positive impact." **—LES BROWN**

One thing I want to get better at:

One step I can take to do that:

One act of kindness I can do today:

One aspiration I have today:

☐ Being healthy & active
☐ Being caring & considerate
☐ Actively engaging with others
☐ Being reflective
☐ Being quiet
☐ Asking for what I need
☐ Other:

DATE: __/__/__

"If you accept the expectations of others, especially negative ones, then you never will change the outcome." —**MICHAEL JORDAN**

One relationship I am neglecting:

One change I can make to improve it:

One beautiful thing I notice:

One happiness I can claim today:

- ☐ Meditation or prayer
- ☐ Exercise
- ☐ Hobby
- ☐ Act of service
- ☐ Act of kindness
- ☐ Being in nature
- ☐ Other:

DATE: __/__/__

"Resilience isn't a single skill. It's a variety of skills and coping mechanisms." —**JEAN CHATZKY**

One hope I have for the future:

One step I can take toward that goal:

One act of service I can provide today:

One aspiration I have today:

- ☐ Being slow & deliberate
- ☐ Being quick & decisive
- ☐ Listening without judging
- ☐ Taking action on ideas
- ☐ Being responsive
- ☐ Being forgiving
- ☐ Other:

"I arise full of eagerness and energy, knowing well what achievement lies ahead of me."
—ZANE GREY

DATE: __/__/__

Best encounter of the week:

One fun thing I want to do this weekend:

One to-do item I want to accomplish:

One person I want to engage with:

"Most of us start out with a positive attitude and a plan to do our best." **—MARILU HENNER**

One thing that is worrying me today:

One step I can take to address my worry:

One thing I am grateful for today:

One aspiration I have today:

- ☐ Patience & understanding
- ☐ Follow-through & accountability
- ☐ Communicating my feelings
- ☐ Allowing discomfort
- ☐ Being vulnerable
- ☐ Taking a risk
- ☐ Other:

DATE: ___/___/___

"It is not how much we have, but how much we enjoy, that makes happiness."
—CHARLES SPURGEON

One relationship that is unsettled:

One change I can make to improve it:

One beautiful thing I notice:

One happiness I can claim today:

☐ Meditation or prayer
☐ Exercise
☐ Hobby
☐ Act of service
☐ Act of kindness
☐ Being in nature
☐ Other:

"With self-discipline most anything is possible."
—THEODORE ROOSEVELT

DATE: __/__/__

One thing I want to get better at:

One step I can take to do that:

One act of kindness I can do today:

One aspiration I have today:

☐ Being healthy & active
☐ Being caring & considerate
☐ Actively engaging with others
☐ Being reflective
☐ Being quiet
☐ Asking for what I need
☐ Other:

DATE: __/__/__

"Positive thinking is a valuable tool that can help you overcome obstacles, deal with pain, and reach new goals." —**AMY MORIN**

One relationship I am neglecting:

One change I can make to improve it:

One beautiful thing I notice:

One happiness I can claim today:

☐ Meditation or prayer
☐ Exercise
☐ Hobby
☐ Act of service
☐ Act of kindness
☐ Being in nature
☐ Other:

DATE: ___/___/___

"Be happy for this moment. This moment is your life." —**OMAR KHAYYAM**

One hope I have for the future:

One step I can take toward that goal:

One act of service I can provide today:

One aspiration I have today:

☐ Being slow & deliberate
☐ Being quick & decisive
☐ Listening without judging
☐ Taking action on ideas
☐ Being responsive
☐ Being forgiving
☐ Other:

"Lord, grant that I may always desire more than I can accomplish." —**MICHELANGELO**

Best encounter of the week:

One fun thing I want to do this weekend:

One to-do item I want to accomplish:

One person I want to engage with:

"When you assume negative intent, you're angry. If you take away that anger an assume positive intent, you will be amazed." **–INDRA NOOYI**

One thing that is worrying me today:

One step I can take to address my worry:

One thing I am grateful for today:

One aspiration I have today:

☐ Patience & understanding
☐ Follow-through & accountability
☐ Communicating my feelings
☐ Allowing discomfort
☐ Being vulnerable
☐ Taking a risk
☐ Other:

"Some cause happiness wherever they go; others whenever they go." —**ANONYMOUS**

DATE: __/__/__

One relationship that is unsettled:

One change I can make to improve it:

One beautiful thing I notice:

One happiness I can claim today:

☐ Meditation or prayer
☐ Exercise
☐ Hobby
☐ Act of service
☐ Act of kindness
☐ Being in nature
☐ Other:

DATE: __/__/__

"It's amazing. Life changes very quickly, in a very positive way, if you let it." **–LINDSEY VONN**

One thing I want to get better at:

One step I can take to do that:

One act of kindness I can do today:

One aspiration I have today:

☐ Being healthy & active
☐ Being caring & considerate
☐ Actively engaging with others
☐ Being reflective
☐ Being quiet
☐ Asking for what I need
☐ Other:

"There is only one happiness in this life, to love and be loved." —**GEORGE SAND**

One relationship I am neglecting:

One change I can make to improve it:

One beautiful thing I notice:

One happiness I can claim today:

- ☐ Meditation or prayer
- ☐ Exercise
- ☐ Hobby
- ☐ Act of service
- ☐ Act of kindness
- ☐ Being in nature
- ☐ Other:

DATE: __/__/__

"Your big opportunity may be right where you are now." —**NAPOLEON HILL**

One hope I have for the future:

One step I can take toward that goal:

One act of service I can provide today:

One aspiration I have today:

- ☐ Being slow & deliberate
- ☐ Being quick & decisive
- ☐ Listening without judging
- ☐ Taking action on ideas
- ☐ Being responsive
- ☐ Being forgiving
- ☐ Other:

DATE: __/__/__

"I am happy to say that everyone that I have met in my life, I have gained something from them."
—WALTER PAYTON

Best encounter of the week:

One fun thing I want to do this weekend:

One to-do item I want to accomplish:

One person I want to engage with:

"Now and then it's good to pause in our pursuit of happiness and just be happy."
—GUILLAUME APOLLINAIRE

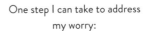

One thing that is worrying
me today:

One step I can take to address
my worry:

One thing I am grateful for today:

One aspiration I have today:

- ☐ Patience & understanding
- ☐ Follow-through & accountability
- ☐ Communicating my feelings
- ☐ Allowing discomfort
- ☐ Being vulnerable
- ☐ Taking a risk
- ☐ Other:

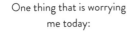

DATE: __/__/__

"In charity there is no excess."
—FRANCIS BACON

One relationship that is unsettled:

One change I can make to improve it:

One beautiful thing I notice:

One happiness I can claim today:

☐ Meditation or prayer
☐ Exercise
☐ Hobby
☐ Act of service
☐ Act of kindness
☐ Being in nature
☐ Other:

"My favorite parable for living a positive and influential life is the Golden Rule: 'Do unto others what you would have them do unto you.'" **—TONY OLLER**

One thing I want to get better at:

One step I can take to do that:

One act of kindness I can do today:

One aspiration I have today:

☐ Being healthy & active
☐ Being caring & considerate
☐ Actively engaging with others
☐ Being reflective
☐ Being quiet
☐ Asking for what I need
☐ Other:

"Happiness grows at our own firesides, and is not to be picked in strangers' gardens."
—DOUGLAS WILLIAM JERROLD

DATE: ___/___/___

One relationship I am neglecting:

One change I can make to improve it:

One beautiful thing I notice:

One happiness I can claim today:

☐ Meditation or prayer
☐ Exercise
☐ Hobby
☐ Act of service
☐ Act of kindness
☐ Being in nature
☐ Other:

"For a gallant spirit there can never be defeat."
—WALLIS SIMPSON

DATE: ___/___/___

One hope I have for the future:

One step I can take toward that goal:

One act of service I can provide today:

One aspiration I have today:

☐ Being slow & deliberate
☐ Being quick & decisive
☐ Listening without judging
☐ Taking action on ideas
☐ Being responsive
☐ Being forgiving
☐ Other:

"I'm a very positive person. My grandmother taught me that happiness is both a skill and a decision, and you are responsible for the outcome."
—HELEN MCCRORY

Best encounter of the week:

One fun thing I want to do this weekend:

One to-do item I want to accomplish:

One person I want to engage with:

"Money can't buy happiness, but it can make you awfully comfortable while you're being miserable."
—CLARE BOOTHE LUCE

DATE: __/__/__

One thing that is worrying me today:

One step I can take to address my worry:

One thing I am grateful for today:

One aspiration I have today:

☐ Patience & understanding
☐ Follow-through & accountability
☐ Communicating my feelings
☐ Allowing discomfort
☐ Being vulnerable
☐ Taking a risk
☐ Other:

DATE: __/__/__

"Once we believe in ourselves, we can risk curiosity, wonder, spontaneous delight, or any experience that reveals the human spirit." —**e. e. cummings**

One relationship that is unsettled:

One change I can make to improve it:

One beautiful thing I notice:

One happiness I can claim today:

☐ Meditation or prayer
☐ Exercise
☐ Hobby
☐ Act of service
☐ Act of kindness
☐ Being in nature
☐ Other:

DATE: __/__/__

"The thing that lies at the foundation of positive change, the way I see it, is service to a fellow human being."—**LECH WALESA**

One thing I want to get better at:

One step I can take to do that:

One act of kindness I can do today:

One aspiration I have today:

- ☐ Being healthy & active
- ☐ Being caring & considerate
- ☐ Actively engaging with others
- ☐ Being reflective
- ☐ Being quiet
- ☐ Asking for what I need
- ☐ Other:

DATE: __/__/__

"Happiness often sneaks in through a door you didn't know you left open." —**JOHN BARRYMORE**

One relationship I am neglecting:

One change I can make to improve it:

One beautiful thing I notice:

One happiness I can claim today:

☐ Meditation or prayer
☐ Exercise
☐ Hobby
☐ Act of service
☐ Act of kindness
☐ Being in nature
☐ Other:

"Only those who have learned the power of sincere and selfless contribution experience life's deepest joy: true fulfillment." **—TONY ROBBINS**

DATE: __/__/__

One hope I have for the future:

One step I can take toward that goal:

One act of service I can provide today:

One aspiration I have today:

☐ Being slow & deliberate
☐ Being quick & decisive
☐ Listening without judging
☐ Taking action on ideas
☐ Being responsive
☐ Being forgiving
☐ Other:

> "*We are all products of our experiences, good and bad. Sometimes you learn as much from the negative experiences as you do from the positive.*"
> —**BRAD GARLINGHOUSE**

Best encounter of the week:

One fun thing I want to do this weekend:

One to-do item I want to accomplish:

One person I want to engage with:

"Try to make at least one person happy every day. If you cannot do a kind deed, speak a kind word. If you cannot speak a kind word, think a kind thought." **—LAWRENCE G. LOVASIK**

One thing that is worrying me today:

One step I can take to address my worry:

One thing I am grateful for today:

One aspiration I have today:

☐ Patience & understanding
☐ Follow-through & accountability
☐ Communicating my feelings
☐ Allowing discomfort
☐ Being vulnerable
☐ Taking a risk
☐ Other:

DATE: __/__/__

"The authentic self is the soul made visible."
—SARAH BAN BREATHNACH

One relationship that is unsettled:

One change I can make to improve it:

One beautiful thing I notice:

One happiness I can claim today:

☐ Meditation or prayer
☐ Exercise
☐ Hobby
☐ Act of service
☐ Act of kindness
☐ Being in nature
☐ Other:

"Winning is fun, but those moments where you can touch someone's life in a very positive way are better." —**TIM HOWARD**

DATE: __/__/__

One thing I want to get better at:

One step I can take to do that:

One act of kindness I can do today:

One aspiration I have today:

☐ Being healthy & active
☐ Being caring & considerate
☐ Actively engaging with others
☐ Being reflective
☐ Being quiet
☐ Asking for what I need
☐ Other:

DATE: ___/___/___

"Cultivate peace and harmony with all."
—GEORGE WASHINGTON

One relationship I am neglecting:

One change I can make to
improve it:

One beautiful thing I notice:

One happiness I can claim today:

☐ Meditation or prayer
☐ Exercise
☐ Hobby
☐ Act of service
☐ Act of kindness
☐ Being in nature
☐ Other:

"Vitality shows in not only the ability to persist but the ability to start over."
—F. SCOTT FITZGERALD

DATE: ___/___/___

One hope I have for the future:

One step I can take toward that goal:

One act of service I can provide today:

One aspiration I have today:

☐ Being slow & deliberate
☐ Being quick & decisive
☐ Listening without judging
☐ Taking action on ideas
☐ Being responsive
☐ Being forgiving
☐ Other:

DATE: __/__/__

"My mother taught me to be honest, to be selfless, and to touch people in a positive way."
—SCOTT EASTWOOD

Best encounter of the week:

One fun thing I want to do this weekend:

One to-do item I want to accomplish:

One person I want to engage with:

"You know it's love when all you want is that person to be happy, even if you're not part of their happiness." —**JULIA ROBERTS**

DATE: __/__/__

One thing that is worrying me today:

One step I can take to address my worry:

One thing I am grateful for today:

One aspiration I have today:

☐ Patience & understanding
☐ Follow-through & accountability
☐ Communicating my feelings
☐ Allowing discomfort
☐ Being vulnerable
☐ Taking a risk
☐ Other:

"*One today is worth two tomorrows.*"
—**BENJAMIN FRANKLIN**

One relationship that is unsettled:

One change I can make to improve it:

One beautiful thing I notice:

One happiness I can claim today:

☐ Meditation or prayer
☐ Exercise
☐ Hobby
☐ Act of service
☐ Act of kindness
☐ Being in nature
☐ Other:

"There is little difference in people, but that little difference makes a big difference. The little difference is attitude. The big difference is whether it's positive or negative." —**W. CLEMENT STONE**

One thing I want to get better at:

One step I can take to do that:

One act of kindness I can do today:

One aspiration I have today:

☐ Being healthy & active
☐ Being caring & considerate
☐ Actively engaging with others
☐ Being reflective
☐ Being quiet
☐ Asking for what I need
☐ Other:

"In order to have great happiness you have to have great pain and unhappiness, otherwise how would you know when you're happy?" **—LESLIE CARON**

DATE: ___/___/___

One relationship I am neglecting:

One change I can make to improve it:

One beautiful thing I notice:

One happiness I can claim today:

☐ Meditation or prayer
☐ Exercise
☐ Hobby
☐ Act of service
☐ Act of kindness
☐ Being in nature
☐ Other:

DATE: __/__/__

"Your heart is full of fertile seeds waiting to sprout." —**MORIHEI UESHIBA**

One hope I have for the future:

One step I can take toward that goal:

One act of service I can provide today:

One aspiration I have today:

☐ Being slow & deliberate
☐ Being quick & decisive
☐ Listening without judging
☐ Taking action on ideas
☐ Being responsive
☐ Being forgiving
☐ Other:

"My house is a very calm and beautiful place and is full of positive energy." **—CHRIS DE BURGH**

Best encounter of the week:

One fun thing I want to do this weekend:

One to-do item I want to accomplish:

One person I want to engage with:

"*Money can't buy you happiness, but it can buy you a yacht big enough to pull up right alongside it.*" —**DAVID LEE ROTH**

DATE: __/__/__

One thing that is worrying me today:

One step I can take to address my worry:

One thing I am grateful for today:

One aspiration I have today:

☐ Patience & understanding
☐ Follow-through & accountability
☐ Communicating my feelings
☐ Allowing discomfort
☐ Being vulnerable
☐ Taking a risk
☐ Other:

DATE: __/__/__

"Love and desire are the spirit's wings to great deeds."
—JOHANN WOLFGANG VON GOETHE

One relationship that is unsettled:

One change I can make to improve it:

One beautiful thing I notice:

One happiness I can claim today:

☐ Meditation or prayer
☐ Exercise
☐ Hobby
☐ Act of service
☐ Act of kindness
☐ Being in nature
☐ Other:

"I really believe in the 'Glow' and live my life that way. It's about being positive inside and out and being the best version of yourself possible." —**TRINITY "NAOMI" FATU**

One thing I want to get better at:

One step I can take to do that:

One act of kindness I can do today:

One aspiration I have today:

☐ Being healthy & active
☐ Being caring & considerate
☐ Actively engaging with others
☐ Being reflective
☐ Being quiet
☐ Asking for what I need
☐ Other:

"*Happiness cannot be traveled to, owned, earned, worn or consumed. Happiness is the spiritual experience of living every minute with love, grace, and gratitude.*" **–DENIS WAITLEY**

One relationship I am neglecting:

One change I can make to improve it:

One beautiful thing I notice:

One happiness I can claim today:

☐ Meditation or prayer
☐ Exercise
☐ Hobby
☐ Act of service
☐ Act of kindness
☐ Being in nature
☐ Other:

"What we need is more people who specialize in the impossible." —**THEODORE ROETHKE**

One hope I have for the future:

One step I can take toward that goal:

One act of service I can provide today:

One aspiration I have today:

☐ Being slow & deliberate
☐ Being quick & decisive
☐ Listening without judging
☐ Taking action on ideas
☐ Being responsive
☐ Being forgiving
☐ Other:

DATE: __/__/__

"It's amazing how a competitive nature can turn a negative into something positive."
—**BARRY MANN**

Best encounter of the week:

One fun thing I want to do this weekend:

One to-do item I want to accomplish:

One person I want to engage with:

"Happiness is not something ready made. It comes from your own actions."
—TENZIN GYATSO, THE 14TH DALAI LAMA

One thing that is worrying me today:

One step I can take to address my worry:

One thing I am grateful for today:

One aspiration I have today:

- ☐ Patience & understanding
- ☐ Follow-through & accountability
- ☐ Communicating my feelings
- ☐ Allowing discomfort
- ☐ Being vulnerable
- ☐ Taking a risk
- ☐ Other:

DATE: ___/___/___

"Great hopes make great men."
—THOMAS FULLER

One relationship that is unsettled:

One change I can make to improve it:

One beautiful thing I notice:

One happiness I can claim today:

☐ Meditation or prayer
☐ Exercise
☐ Hobby
☐ Act of service
☐ Act of kindness
☐ Being in nature
☐ Other:

DATE: __/__/__

"How do you nurture a positive attitude when all the statistics say you're a dead man? You go to work." **–PATRICK SWAYZE**

One thing I want to get better at:

One step I can take to do that:

One act of kindness I can do today:

One aspiration I have today:

☐ Being healthy & active
☐ Being caring & considerate
☐ Actively engaging with others
☐ Being reflective
☐ Being quiet
☐ Asking for what I need
☐ Other:

"An effort made for the happiness of others lifts us above ourselves." —**LYDIA M. CHILD**

DATE: __/__/__

One relationship I am neglecting:

One change I can make to improve it:

One beautiful thing I notice:

One happiness I can claim today:

☐ Meditation or prayer
☐ Exercise
☐ Hobby
☐ Act of service
☐ Act of kindness
☐ Being in nature
☐ Other:

DATE: __/__/__

"We relish news of our heroes, forgetting that we are extraordinary to somebody too."
—HELEN HAYES

One hope I have for the future:

One step I can take toward that goal:

One act of service I can provide today:

One aspiration I have today:

☐ Being slow & deliberate
☐ Being quick & decisive
☐ Listening without judging
☐ Taking action on ideas
☐ Being responsive
☐ Being forgiving
☐ Other:

"Frustration, although quite painful at times, is a very positive and essential part of success."
—BO BENNETT

DATE: __/__/__

Best encounter of the week:

One fun thing I want to do this weekend:

One to-do item I want to accomplish:

One person I want to engage with:

DATE: ___/___/___

"Happiness is dependent on self-discipline. We are the biggest obstacles to our own happiness. It is much easier to do battle with society and with others than to fight our own nature."
—DENNIS PRAGER

One thing that is worrying me today:

One step I can take to address my worry:

One thing I am grateful for today:

One aspiration I have today:

☐ Patience & understanding
☐ Follow-through & accountability
☐ Communicating my feelings
☐ Allowing discomfort
☐ Being vulnerable
☐ Taking a risk
☐ Other:

DATE: __/__/__

"Live your beliefs and you can turn the world around." —**HENRY DAVID THOREAU**

One relationship that is unsettled:

One change I can make to improve it:

One beautiful thing I notice:

One happiness I can claim today:

☐ Meditation or prayer
☐ Exercise
☐ Hobby
☐ Act of service
☐ Act of kindness
☐ Being in nature
☐ Other:

DATE: ___/___/___

"I have learned that champions aren't just born; champions can be made when they embrace and commit to life-changing positive habits."
—LEWIS HOWES

One thing I want to get better at:

One step I can take to do that:

One act of kindness I can do today:

One aspiration I have today:

- ☐ Being healthy & active
- ☐ Being caring & considerate
- ☐ Actively engaging with others
- ☐ Being reflective
- ☐ Being quiet
- ☐ Asking for what I need
- ☐ Other:

"Happiness is a virtue, not its reward."
—BARUCH SPINOZA

DATE: ___/___/___

One relationship I am neglecting:

One change I can make to improve it:

One beautiful thing I notice:

One happiness I can claim today:

☐ Meditation or prayer
☐ Exercise
☐ Hobby
☐ Act of service
☐ Act of kindness
☐ Being in nature
☐ Other:

"The only thing that ultimately matters is to eat an ice cream cone, play a slide trombone, plant a small tree; good God, now you're free."
—RAY MANZAREK

One hope I have for the future:

One step I can take toward that goal:

One act of service I can provide today:

One aspiration I have today:

- ☐ Being slow & deliberate
- ☐ Being quick & decisive
- ☐ Listening without judging
- ☐ Taking action on ideas
- ☐ Being responsive
- ☐ Being forgiving
- ☐ Other:

DATE: __/__/__

"A positive atmosphere nurtures a positive attitude, which is required to take positive action."
—**RICHARD M. DEVOS**

Best encounter of the week:

One fun thing I want to do this weekend:

One to-do item I want to accomplish:

One person I want to engage with:

DATE: __/__/__

It is not easy to find happiness in ourselves, and it is not possible to find it elsewhere."
—AGNES REPPLIER

One thing that is worrying me today:

One step I can take to address my worry:

One thing I am grateful for today:

One aspiration I have today:

☐ Patience & understanding
☐ Follow-through & accountability
☐ Communicating my feelings
☐ Allowing discomfort
☐ Being vulnerable
☐ Taking a risk
☐ Other:

"You are always free to change your mind and choose a different future or a different past."
—RICHARD BACH

DATE: __/__/__

One relationship that is unsettled:

One change I can make to improve it:

One beautiful thing I notice:

One happiness I can claim today:

☐ Meditation or prayer
☐ Exercise
☐ Hobby
☐ Act of service
☐ Act of kindness
☐ Being in nature
☐ Other:

DATE: __/__/__

"Better to be called something positive and inspirational than something negative."
—DONNIE YEN

One thing I want to get better at:

One step I can take to do that:

One act of kindness I can do today:

One aspiration I have today:

- ☐ Being healthy & active
- ☐ Being caring & considerate
- ☐ Actively engaging with others
- ☐ Being reflective
- ☐ Being quiet
- ☐ Asking for what I need
- ☐ Other:

"Most folks are about as happy as they make up their minds to be." —**ABRAHAM LINCOLN**

One relationship I am neglecting:

One change I can make to improve it:

One beautiful thing I notice:

One happiness I can claim today:

☐ Meditation or prayer
☐ Exercise
☐ Hobby
☐ Act of service
☐ Act of kindness
☐ Being in nature
☐ Other:

"Faith is love taking the form of aspiration."
—WILLIAM ELLERY CHANNING

One hope I have for the future:

One step I can take toward that goal:

One act of service I can provide today:

One aspiration I have today:

☐ Being slow & deliberate
☐ Being quick & decisive
☐ Listening without judging
☐ Taking action on ideas
☐ Being responsive
☐ Being forgiving
☐ Other:

A YEAR IN REVIEW

DATE: __/__/__

LOOKING BACK OVER THE LAST YEAR . . .

What gave me the most joy?

What am I most proud of accomplishing?

What do I feel ready to take on now?

Why?

CONTRIBUTORS

Adams, Amy—Am. actress

Aeschylus—Ancient Greek playwright

Aesop—Ancient Greek fabulist & storyteller

Alda, Alan—Am. actor

Alexander the Great—Ancient Macedonian king

Ali, Muhammad—Am. prizefighter

Allen, George, Sr.—Am. football coach

Angelou, Maya—Am. author

Apollinaire, Guillaume—Fr. poet

Aquinas, Thomas—13th-cen. Ital. theologian

Arjun, Allu—Indian actor

Armstrong, Kristin—Am. cyclist

Armstrong, Neil—Am. astronaut

Ash, Mary Kay—Am. businesswoman

Aucoin, Kevyn—Am. makeup artist

Bach, Richard—Am. writer

Bacon, Francis—16th-cen. Eng. philosopher

Bailey, David—Eng. photographer

Baker, Ella—Am. activist

Ball, Lonzo—Am. basketball player

Ballou, Hosea—18th-cen. Am. theologist

Ban Breathnach, Sarah—Am. author

Banks, Tyra—TV host & model

Barr, Amelia—19th-cen. Eng. writer

Barrymore, John—Am. actor

Beck, Martha—Am. author

Beecher, Henry Ward—19th-cen. Am. clergyman

Begley, Sharon—Am. journalist

Bennett, Bo—Am. swimmer

Berle, Milton—Am. comedian

Bey, Yaslin—Am. rapper

Bieber, Justin—Can. singer

Boggs, Wade—Am. baseball player

Brahms, Johannes—19th-cen. Ger. composer

Bronfman, Hannah—Am. entrepreneur

Brothers, Joyce—Am. psychologist

Brown, H. Jackson, Jr.—Am. author

Brown, Les—Am. author

Browning, Elizabeth Barrett—19th-cen. Eng. poet

Browning, Robert—19th-cen. Eng. poet

Bryant, Kobe—Am. basketball player

Bryant, Paul "Bear"—Am. football coach

Buddha—Founder of Buddhism

Buffett, Warren—Am. business magnate

Burnett, Carol—Am. entertainer

Butler, Octavia E.—Am. author

Cameron, Matt—Am. musician

Campbell, Joseph—Am. author

Canfield, Jack—Am. author

Carlyle, Thomas—19th-cen. Scot. historian

Caron, Leslie—Fr.-Am. actress

Cerf, Bennett—Am. publisher

Channing, William Ellery—19th-cen. Am. theologian

Chatzky, Jean—Am. journalist

Child, Lydia M.—19th-cen. Am. abolitionist

Chopra, Deepak—Indian-Am. author

Thurchill, Winston—Brit. prime minister

Clarke, Arthur C.—Brit. author

Clay, Bryan—Am. decathlete

Clemens, Roger—Am. baseball player

Clinton, Hillary—US secretary of state

Coelho, Paulo—Brazilian novelist

Comaneci, Nadia—Romanian gymnast

Cook, Robert A.—Am. minister

Copeland, Bill—Am. poet

Copernicus, Nicolaus—14th-cen. Polish mathematician

Covey, Stephen—Am. educator and author

cummings, e. e.—Am. poet

de Burgh, Chris—Brit.-Irish singer-songwriter

Dean, Jimmy—Am. country singer

DeGeneres, Ellen—Am. comedian

Democritus—Ancient Greek philosopher

Dempsey, Jack—Am. professional boxer

Desae, Tena—Indian actress

DeVos, Richard MT—Am. entrepreneur

Disney, Walt—Am. entrepreneur

Disraeli, Benjamin—19th-cen. Brit. statesman

Dorsett, Tony—Am. football player

Douglas, Tommy—Can. politician

Eastwood, Scott—Am. actor

Einstein, Albert—Ger.-Am. physicist

Eliot, George—19th-cen. Eng. writer

Emerson, Ralph Waldo—19th-cen. Am. essayist & philosopher

Epictetus—Ancient Greek philosopher

Erasmus, Desiderius—16th-cen. Dutch philosopher

Evans, Richard L.—Am. missionary

Fatu, Trinity "Naomi"—Am. professional wrestler

Faust, James E.—Am. religious leader

Fierstein, Harvey—Am. actor

ABOUT THE AUTHOR

LEAHANNE THOMAS creates and invents tools to help people live happier and more fulfilling lives. She advises, counsels, and coaches people through transitions and changes. She lives with her family in Maryland. Visit her at www.ltcoachings.com.